Le Désert de Retz

1. "The House of the Désert, belonging to Mr. de Monville."

Le Désert de Retz

A Late Eighteenth-Century French Folly Garden,
The Artful Landscape of Monsieur de Monville

Diana Ketcham

A history of this landscape garden and its twenty architectural monuments, including the legendary false ruin, La Colonne Détruite, from its origins on the eve of the French Revolution to its restoration two centuries later; illustrated with historical views of the park and related sites, the twenty-six engravings of the Désert in *Jardins anglo-chinois à la mode* of Le Rouge from 1785, and photographs of the grounds and follies from 1850 to 1993.

The MIT Press
Cambridge, Massachusetts
London, England

First MIT Press edition, 1994

This book was set in Cochin by DEKR Corporation and was printed and bound in the United States of America.

Library of Congress Cataloging-in-Publication Data

Ketcham, Diana.
  Le Désert de Retz : a late eighteenth-century French folly garden
: the artful landscape of Monsieur de Monville / Diana Ketcham.
    p. cm.
  Includes bibliographical references (p.   ) and index.
  ISBN 0-262-11186-1
  1. Désert de Retz (Chambourcy, France) 2. Monville, François
Nicolas Henri Racine de, 1734–1797—Homes and haunts—France—
Chambourcy. 3. Gardens, English—France—Chambourcy. I. Title.
SB466.F83D474 1994
712'.6'0944366—dc20   93-50749
                                                          CIP

Frontispiece. "The House of the Désert, belonging to Mr. de Monville." This 1808 view of the Broken Column, published approximately thirty years after its construction, shows the jagged roofline and cracked walls that caused the royal gardener Thomas Blaikie to say of Monville, "I cannot think but that he meant to imitate the Tower of Babel." The Cross of St. Andrew, a Masonic symbol, can be seen on the roof. A. L. J. de Laborde, *Descriptions des nouveaux jardins de la France, et des ses anciens châteaux*, Paris, 1808–1815. Engraving. *Coll:* G. B. Carson.

Contents

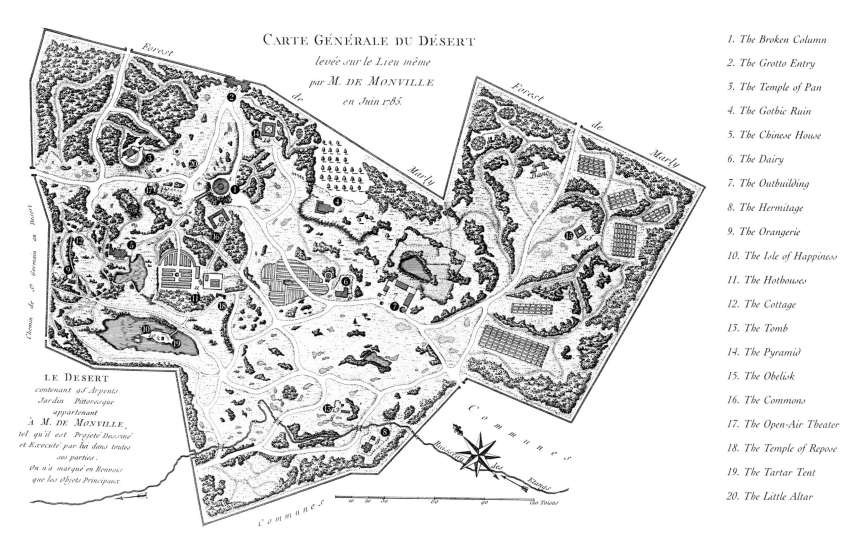

CARTE GÉNÉRALE DU DÉSERT
levée sur le Lieu même
par M. DE MONVILLE
en Juin 1785.

LE DESERT
contenant 95 Arpents.
Jardin Pittoresque
appartenant
À M. DE MONVILLE,
tel qu'il est Projeté Dessiné
et Exécuté par lui dans toutes
ses parties.
On n'a marqué en Renvois
que les Objets Principaux.

1. *The Broken Column*

2. *The Grotto Entry*

3. *The Temple of Pan*

4. *The Gothic Ruin*

5. *The Chinese House*

6. *The Dairy*

7. *The Outbuilding*

8. *The Hermitage*

9. *The Orangerie*

10. *The Isle of Happiness*

11. *The Hothouses*

12. *The Cottage*

13. *The Tomb*

14. *The Pyramid*

15. *The Obelisk*

16. *The Commons*

17. *The Open-Air Theater*

18. *The Temple of Repose*

19. *The Tartar Tent*

20. *The Little Altar*

GENERAL MAP OF THE DÉSERT DE RETZ
From *Détails de nouveaux jardins à la mode: Jardins anglo-chinois*
(Paris: G. L. Le Rouge, 1776-1787)

2. An adaptation of the 1785 engraved map published by Georges Le Rouge in his volume devoted to the Désert de Retz, showing the location of seventeen follies. The meadow and farm area to the bottom and right is the site of the golf course.

Acknowledgments

Le Désert de Retz was first published by the Arion Press, San Francisco, in 1990, in a limited edition of 400 copies. This revised and expanded edition has been redesigned and published by the MIT Press with the permission of Arion Press.

The author wishes to thank G. B. Carson, whose collection of graphic and written material about the Désert de Retz was the resource for development of the project, and Olivier Choppin de Janvry, who wrote the afterword, which was translated from the French by Diana Ketcham. The author is grateful to the following individuals and institutions for permission to reproduce illustrations that appear in this book: Achenbach Foundation for Graphic Arts, San Francisco; Denise Bellon, Paris; Bibliothèque Nationale, Paris; Marion Brenner, Berkeley; Getty Center for the History of Art and the Humanities, Santa Monica; G. B. Carson, Berkeley; Michael Kenna, San Francisco; Massachusetts Historical Society, Boston; Olivier Choppin de Janvry and Société Civile du Désert de Retz, Paris; National Swedish Art Museums, Royal Academy, and Royal Library, Stockholm; Roger-Viollet, Paris; University of Virginia Library, Charlottesville; and to Arthur Danto, Judd Hubert, Donlyn Lyndon, Basil Guy, Linda Fletcher, and Eric Haskell for reading the text.

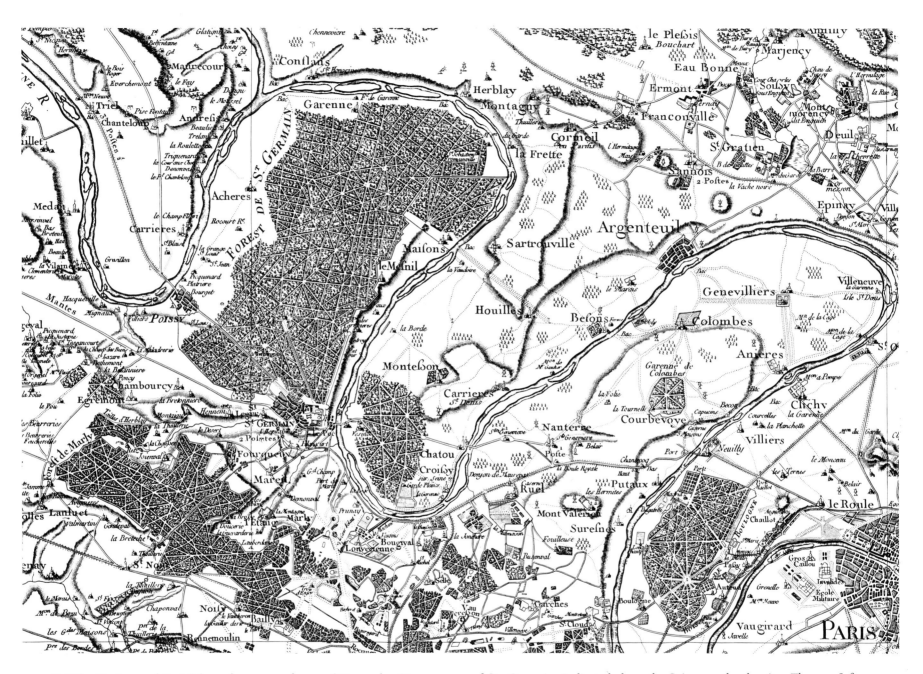

3. "The Environs of Paris" from the engraved map of France by César-François Cassini de Thury, Paris, 1755–1789. The village of Retz appears in the lower left-hand section, on the northern border of the Forest of Marly, west of St. Germain and directly south of Chambourcy. An area called "le Désert" is marked to the east of Retz in the direction of St. Germain. Indicated along the Seine are the the sites Thomas Jefferson mentions visiting on his way to see the Désert de Retz in 1786: the Pont de Neuilly, the Machine of Marly, Louveciennes, and St. Germain. The related gardens of Bagatelle and the Parc Monceau are marked on the western edge of Paris.

Le Désert de Retz

Twelve miles from the heart of Paris, one of the glories of the architecture of fantasy has lain forgotten for two hundred years. The Désert de Retz was built as the private pleasure garden of François Nicolas Henri Racine de Monville, a gentleman of fashion during the reigns of Louis XV and Louis XVI. Created on the eve of the Revolution, between 1774 and 1789, the garden was dismantled a few years later. But over the period of fifteen years, and within the confines of one hundred acres, its owner realized a complete world in miniature. Monsieur de Monville's world was remarkable in being both uniquely his own and a reflection of his society. It attempted to "unite in a single garden all times and all places,"[1] with the continents of Africa, Asia, and America represented by their native plants and the history of world architecture recapitulated in twenty follies. Laid out according to the Enlightenment categories of learning in natural science, architecture, and history, its atmosphere was nevertheless eccentric, bizarre even, making it a rare instance of what recent historians call the psychological garden of the late eighteenth century.

Monville was imitating other picturesque gardens when he set up a model farm, dairy, and orangerie within a natural-looking park. He followed fashion in ornamenting his landscape with fanciful architectural structures, or follies, in classical, oriental, Egyptian, and Gothic styles. But Monville endowed his creation with one feature so imaginative as to place it radically outside convention. This was the "Colonne Détruite," or Broken Column, regarded as the most extraordinary folly in Europe, a four-story habitation in the shape of a ruined column, its walls riven by fissures and its roof a jagged line. With its awesome scale and intimations of violence near at hand, Monville's Column put visitors in mind of the terrible history of the Tower of Babel. As one observer of the period, the Prince de Ligne, wrote, its size "gives the impression of a height great enough to incur God's wrath, as did the tower of his first children".[2]

In its glory, M. de Monville's garden attracted such visitors as Thomas Jefferson, who used elements of the floor plan of the Broken Column in his design for the University of Virginia rotunda. King Gustavus III of Sweden made a pilgrimage there in preparation for remaking his gardens at Haga and

Drottningholm, and likewise borrowed from the Column. The Désert was a favorite retreat of Madame du Barry, the Duc d'Orléans, and Queen Marie Antoinette, who found inspiration there for her English gardens at the Petit Trianon at Versailles. The painters Hubert Robert, Vigée-Lebrun, and Carmontelle inspected Monville's wonders firsthand, as did scores of curious citizens, to whom the proprietor issued tickets at the gate, requiring only that visitors be decently dressed. More than a century later, in decay, the Désert would excite the imaginations of the Surrealists. André Breton and his group climbed the walls of the Désert and posed for photographs before the Broken Column. Jacques Prévert appropriated Izis's photos of the folly's ruined interior for the making of a collage. Abel Gance filmed in the overgrown park. And among the literary, Colette, Cyril Connolly, and Hans Arp paid tribute to the magic of the Désert.

In our own time, what is most astonishing about Monville's Désert is its survival. It is the only one of the folly gardens of France's late eighteenth century that still exists in close to its original state, from a long list that includes Lunéville, Ermenonville, Cassan, Chantilly, Bagatelle, Raincy, Rambouillet, Chanteloup, Bonnelles, Menars, La Folie Saint James, Monceau, Méréville, and Betz. Their precursor, the fabulous folly garden of Moulin-Joli, was leveled after the Revolution. For most, the years have brought renovation of the buildings and the subdivision of the gardens, leaving little sense of the original scheme. Of some of the grandest, only architectural fragments remain: the Chinese pavilion at Cassan, the Pyramid and Cascade at the Parc Monceau in Paris, the Pagoda at Chanteloup, and the Temple of Modern Philosophy at Ermenonville. Decades of neglect saved the Désert de Retz from this common fate. Forgotten or ignored by a series of absentee owners, the park and its architectural contents were permitted to decay undisturbed and were taken up only in the 1980s as the object of restoration.

The result is that what the eighteenth century devised as an artificial ruin became in the twentieth century a literal one, an irony whose poignancy has moved all of those who have pushed through the underbrush to enter into this forgotten place. The sight awaiting them was like a blurred photograph of the original. The essential outlines of Monville's landscaping remained, as did the Broken Column and five of the lesser follies, their character both softened and intensified by time.

Coming upon the Désert de Retz in the 1940s, Osvald Sirén was astonished to find that

> The wall is for the most part still intact, as are also the huge stone blocks of the north gate. . . . So exuberant is the vegetation that . . . the unsuspecting stranger, who enters the place by the narrow and traffic-worn village street, if he has not an observant eye, may easily pass the main building without discovering it. Covered with creepers that grow even through the windows, and possessing to a remarkable degree the atmosphere of the Castle of the Sleeping Beauty, though a castle sans princess. The impression that the building is half buried is now even stronger than it was originally, thanks to the luxuriant growth of the surrounding trees and bushes. At the same time the encroachments of the vegetation conceal the worst evidences of the neglect that has allowed the building to fall into a state of ruin beyond that which its contriver ever intended.[3]

The Castle of Sleeping Beauty, the secret garden, the place time forgot—such were the story-book images the Désert could evoke for the literary minded. Colette, who began frequenting the Désert in the 1930s, embraced it as a proof of nature's inevitable triumph. For her, the unfettered growth of plants and trees had carried out the architect's morbid intentions, creating an atmosphere of sublime decay. "As it leaves its high water mark of vegetation on Retz and obliterates the presence of its indifferent and discouraged owners, June exceeds hope and completes the work of Racine de Monville, who wanted the new to be struck down and his saplings turned into hundred-year-old trees. There is neither scything nor pruning at Retz. Few of us realize the power of vegetal life in soil enriched by the fall of dead leaves, by the annual soaking of the grass. Retz's luxuriance is that of a dream, of a fantastic tale, of an imaginary island."[4]

The Désert owes its poignancy also to its moment in French history. Both the garden and its owner were creatures of the Ancien Régime, and perished with it. Completed as the Revolution was approaching, Monville's garden was taken over by the republican government in 1792, its precious furnishings and rare plants sold at public sales or appropriated by the state museums. Five years later, Monville died at the age of sixty-three, of his excesses as the saying goes, having only by chance eluded the grim end of his royal friends.[5]

As a garden in the natural style, Monville's Désert was by definition perishable. It could not aspire to permanence, as had the formal, architectural gardens of the previous era. Whereas the plan of the seventeenth-century garden was derived from the rules of geometry, its regular lines reinforced by paths and terraces of stone, its successor was shaped in apparently artless fashion from plants themselves, to look as if it had emerged from the surrounding countryside. And into the landscape it could return if neglected.

Fragile, too, was the social position of the wealthy amateurs who were the greatest enthusiasts of the picturesque garden in France. The grand garden style perfected by Le Nôtre in the seventeenth century had been the instrument of monarchy. With it, Louis XIV had asserted the exalted status of the Bourbon kings, enshrining his court in a man-made landscape whose proportions alone were sufficient to inspire awe. At Versailles, 240 acres of gardens were set in a park of 4,000 acres, within a hunting forest of 15,000, and enclosed by a wall 26 miles long.

By the time Monville had embarked on his garden in the 1770s, no one could dream of creating on this scale: not the monarchs, who had depleted the treasury with vast building projects and foreign wars, and certainly not the minor nobility or private citizens like Monville. The creator of the Désert knew that the era of the great parks was over. It is an aspect of the wit of his undertaking that by comparison with the royal domains Monville's is a mere dot on the landscape. Yet by proximity it puts itself on the same level of importance as Versailles, Rambouillet, and Marly, even to the point of incorporating the forest and vistas of the latter as its own. One may think of Monville in modern terms as an appropriation artist, who created his own views by reusing the landscapes designed for his royal neighbors.

As an exercise in park design in small, the Désert de Retz exaggerates and ingeniously fuses two enthusiasms that had reached their height by the third quarter of the eighteenth century: the picturesque garden, and the pavilion, or small country house on the grounds of a grand château. In its park and architecture, Monville's Désert is a textbook example of the picturesque garden in its "anglo-chinois" vein, which was characterized by irregular landscaping and the presence of follies, or *fabriques* as they were commonly called in France. The term had originally carried the meaning of "any building in a painting," hence the *fabrique*'s function as the focal point of a composed vista, whose literary and historical allusions were meant to move the viewer to salutary states of awe, melancholy, joy, or terror.[6] The twenty follies at the Désert were representative of the architectural periods and styles of the comparable gardens of Moulin-Joli, Ermenonville, Bagatelle, Monceau, and Méréville. Lacking were a mill and a philosopher's hut, but there were two classical ruins (the Temple of Pan and the Broken Column), a medieval ruin (the Gothic Church), a classical temple (the Temple of Repose), a Chinese pavilion, a Tartar tent, an obelisk, a pyramid, a tomb, a rustic bridge, a thatched-roof cottage, a hermitage, a dairy, an open-air theater, and a grotto (the Marly entry).

Of these, the Broken Column is a folly in its appearance, but a pavilion in size and function. Characteristically, Monville reverses the customary hierarchies of scale, making his pavilion the largest building in the park and setting it on a hill where it loomed over his temples. Although, in a literal sense, the Broken Column draws from many cultural motifs of the period, including the iconography of Freemasonry, it is most striking for the unexpected way it alters them. Its strangeness sets the Désert apart from the comparable gardens of the epoch. Not that the theme of the ruined classical column was not a favorite among builders of false ruins. It was a common feature in the landscape paintings that influenced practitioners of the picturesque garden. At Betz, designed in the mid-1780s by Hubert Robert, a round tower with dramatically cracked walls was retained as a folly. In the unbuilt schemes of the visionary architect Boullée, the truncated column is one of the classical elements rendered in overscale. But nothing actually built in Europe in the eighteenth century rivals Monville's Broken Column, in either its size or the boldness of its conception.

For the architectural centerpiece of his domain, Monville took the conceit of the false ruin to a surreal extreme. Standing fifty feet tall, it appears from a distance to be the base of a column that once supported a classical temple. But a temple built by whom? Not humans surely. The proportions force upon us the sensation that we are Lilliputian inhabitants of a countryside overrun by giants, and not benign ones, either. For it was presumably they whose violent undertakings brought the temple down. As Swift knew, such tinkerings with scale generate the anxious atmosphere of the fairy tale and set the stage for terror.

Among landscape artists of the period, miniaturization was the favored technique for creating a mood of altered reality.

This was the sensibility that reduced temples to the scale of garden sheds. In his Broken Column, Monville applied this principle relentlessly and in reverse. Instead of shrinking a monument, he giganticized a fragment thereof. The oddness of the effect can hardly be overstated. In the conventional picturesque garden, the presence of follies enhances the viewers' sense of physical and intellectual power, placing them in a controlling relation to the architecture of all times and all places, which has been scaled down to the comfortable proportions of the rural vernacular. As stated by the theorists, the goal is to ennoble the everyday landscape. In practice it also has the reassuring effect of domesticating the noble. But there is nothing cozy about the picturesqueness of the Désert. Here it is the viewer who is reduced, rendered small and bewildered before the mysterious bulk of the Broken Column. In the boldness of its violation of conventions of scale, Monville's Broken Column sets the mood of the entire park. It stands like a sinister beacon, signaling the visitor to prepare for an encounter with the bizarre.

Horace Walpole observed that one of the ways the French differed from the English was in their habit of using garden architecture rather than only looking at it.[7] Monville furthered this tendency by actually living in his follies, first in the Chinese Pavilion, built in 1777, and after 1781 in the Broken Column. In the case of the Column, the crude and fantastical exterior belied the refinement of the space within, which offered all the amenities of an aristocrat's country retreat. As such, the Broken Column belongs to that flowering of pavilion architecture that marked the end of the Ancien Régime, when, fatigued by the relentless etiquette of the court at Versailles, the nobles found it necessary to get away. The monarchs themselves had been the first to flee, and to consecrate a distinguished architecture to the process. From the time Louis XIV commissioned the architect Louis Le Vau's Trianon de Porcelaine in 1661, through the construction of such jewel-box habitations as the Grand

Trianon, Pavillon Français, Petit Trianon, Pavillon Du Barry Louveciennes, the Hermitage of Madame Pompadour, and Bagatelle, the pavilions were associated with the royal mistresses and the rites of intimacy. It was to the Petit Trianon that Louis XV would slip away to pass an entire day with Pompadour, having told his retinue he was going hunting. There the monarch would amuse himself by brewing his own coffee and preparing little meals in the chafing dish, or would relax with his embroidery.

Monville would have known the royal pavilions and their role as *maisons de rendez-vous*. When he came to build his own retreat, he retained their hedonistic function, while departing absolutely from the restrained classicism of their architecture. Was Monville implicated in the decadence of this style of country life? Perhaps the charge of *sybaritisme*, in his warrant of arrest in the Terror, could be traced to his reputation as one who escaped to the country in the style of Pompadour, Du Barry, and Marie Antoinette, to whose detractors the pavilions symbolized their most inane extravagances.

The royal pavilions stood witness to the desperate final dramas of these mistresses of leisure. It was in the grotto of the Petit Trianon that Queen Marie Antoinette sought futile refuge from the mob that had come to take her to Paris, and eventually to prison and the guillotine. Her arch-rival Du Barry was captured at Louveciennes, the site of the exquisite pavilion built for her and Louis XV by Ledoux. The ill-fated Princess de Lamballe, companion of the rustic amusements of Marie Antoinette and daughter of the builder of a much-imitated early pavilion, the Cottage at Rambouillet, was snatched from her friend's side to have her head placed on a pike in front of the Temple, a sobering spectacle for the queen as she later gazed out from her prison cell.[8]

The annals of the Terror associate the creator of the Désert de Retz with the last moments of the royal family. The best-known anecdote that has come down to us regarding Monville recounts a conversation with the king's cousin the Duc d'Orléans, then calling himself "Philippe Egalité," and soon to be named *compagnon de plaisir*, of Monville in the latter's arrest warrant. A testimony to Monville's reputation as a worldling and wit, the story tells how he was dining with his friend the duke on the evening of April 6, 1793, when a messenger arrived with news that the nobleman's arrest had been voted by the Convention. As the sole was being served, the duke railed against the ingratitude of the revolutionaries, no doubt recalling that to please them he had voted for the execution of his cousin Louis XVI.

"It is terrible, my lord, but what can you expect?" Monville is said to have replied. "They have gotten all they want from your highness and are simply doing with you what I am doing with this lemon squeezed of all its juice," he said, tossing the lemon rind into the fire and telling the duke to eat his sole before it got cold.[9]

Enthusiasm for the aesthetic embodied in the Désert de Retz did not survive the Revolution. By the beginning of the next century, opinion of Monville's taste had fallen very low. Laborde dismissed it in his 1808 *Descriptions des Nouveaux Jardins de la France*, as "having once had a great reputation."[10] He singled out the Chinese House, which Monville's contemporary the Prince de Ligne had praised as worthy of "being acknowledged by the Emperor of China himself,"[11] as "an example of the bad taste that reigned at the time and the great expense caused by such a detestable kind of magnificence."[12]

But let us turn to a happier time—that September day in 1786 when the Désert received a visit from Thomas Jefferson and the English painter Maria Cosway. Jefferson was then in the second of his five years as minister to France. His wife Martha had died four years before, leaving Jefferson to seek consolation in the study of architecture and the pursuit of love, both undertaken with the zest for which he was famous. In his romance with Maria Cosway, he united these two enterprises, enlisting this cultivated Italian-born artist in his inspection of the latest developments in French architecture and horticulture. A painter who exhibited yearly at the Royal Academy in London, she had come to Paris with her husband, the English miniaturist Richard Cosway, who was engaged to paint the portraits of the Duc d'Orléans's children.

Maria Cosway was the type of woman Jefferson warmed to; refined and fastidious like his wife, she possessed a vivacity that sustained her reputation as a beauty into her thirties, when she became the companion of Jefferson's travels. Their trip to the Désert is the subject of his ardent remembrance in a love letter entitled a "dialogue between my Head and my Heart," a reference to his misgivings about falling in love with a married woman. When they were together at the Désert, however, Jefferson's conscience must have been on holiday. For he writes of that day in words of unqualified rapture. "How gay did the face of nature appear," he recalled. "Hills, valleys, châteaux, gardens, rivers, every object wore its liveliest hue. Whence did they borrow it? From the presence of our charming companion."[13]

On that late summer morning, Thomas Jefferson and Maria Cosway would have set out from his rented house at the corner of the Champs Elysées and the rue de Berri, the Hôtel de Langeac, which commanded a wide view of the city. As they mounted the boulevard going west, they could have looked across the Seine at one of Jefferson's favorite Paris sights, the construction of the Hôtel de Salm, now the Palais de la Légion d'Honneur, which was to influence his remodeling of Monticello. That day, they were on their way to examine another architectural experiment whose principles Jefferson would apply at home. Monville's Broken Column would so impress the American that he would imitate its curvilinear floor plan in an unbuilt scheme for a capitol building in Washington and in the University of Virginia rotunda (figures 14–15).[14]

As they crossed the Pont de Neuilly and followed the Seine westward, the couple would have been taking a route popular with English and American sightseers, the bustling road connecting Paris with the royal residences at Versailles, Rambouillet, Louveciennes, Marly, Saint-Germain-en-Laye, and Saint Cloud. Near the town of Louveciennes, where they stopped for lunch, they would have passed the Machine of Marly, the moving ladder that carried water up from the Seine to supply the fountains and drinking water of Versailles and the Château of Marly. Jefferson would have been riveted by the sight of this engineering marvel. Recalling their drive to Saint Germain-en-Laye, where they looked back over the Seine Valley toward the spires of Paris, Jefferson exclaimed, "How beautiful was every object, the Pont de Neuilly, the hills along the Seine, the rainbows of the machine of Marly, the terraces of St. Germain, the châteaux, the gardens, the statues of Marly, the Pavilion of Lucienne. Recollect, too, Madrid, Bagatelle, the King's Garden, the Dessert [sic]."

At Marly, Jefferson would surely have paused to examine the park. We know that its layout, with two rows of pavilions flanking the Château, influenced his campus at the University of Virginia.[15] Entering the Forest of Marly, they would have taken the road that gave Monville privileged access across royal land. At the stone wall marking the edge of the Forest, a wooden gate with diamond-shaped panels announced their arrival at the Désert de Retz.

On the other side, Jefferson and his companion found themselves in a different world. They would have entered through two plain wooden doors, to emerge from a grotto of jagged rocks, where a pair of satyrs brandishing torches stood welcome. That the rocks were made from plaster and the satyrs cut from tin was the sign that they had passed from nature's countryside into the realm of art.

Across the valley was another astonishing sight, a gigantic classical column broken off at the top. "How grand the idea excited by the remains of such a column," Jefferson pronounced in his letter to Cosway. To the left stood structures in a less outlandish vein of fantasy, a ruined Gothic church and a pyramid; to the right, a Doric temple. A narrow path curved down the hill to the south wall, passing clumps of young cedars, beeches, and lindens. From here the visitors could have looked out over a cheerful panorama of farmlands to the Abbey of Joyenval, which Monville had appropriated as the focus of one of his views.

Here at the base of his little valley Monville had created two lakes. One reflected the sinuous outlines of the Chinese House, crafted in teak stained violet and blue, with curving roofs and bell-shaped chimneys. On an island in the other lake stood the Tartar Tent, cut from tin and gay with painted stripes. Turning back toward the Broken Column, they would have passed the Little Altar, with a tipped urn balanced on top, and the Open-Air Theater, a stone stage sheltered by elms. In the distance to the right, there would be glimpses of the Obelisk, the columns of the Temple of Repose, and the simple buildings of the Dairy and Farm. From the dell was another of the Désert's dramatic views, across a great meadow toward the white bulk of the Column. Ascending the rise toward the house, the visitors may have been met by their host, appearing suddenly above them on the the rustic bridge, or silhouetted against the opening of the tunnel leading into the Column's cellar (figures 5–12).

Imagine Jefferson coming upon the Broken Column. He would have been struck by the ingenuity with which a four-story house had been concealed within this round tower. Of its three rows of windows—square, rectangular, and oval—the lowest was obscured by shrubbery. A set of upper windows was hidden behind the cracks in the walls, created to further the illusion that the structure had been blasted by God's wrath. This architectural sleight-of-hand must have delighted the designer of Monticello, which is similarly a virtuoso effort to make a

multi-level house look like one story from outside. Jefferson was less successful than Monville in disguising his windows, however. Guests at Monticello would complain of the awkwardness of bedroom windows that rose only a short distance above the floor, in an effort to make the upper story appear to be part of the one below.[16]

We know that Jefferson went inside, where he was intrigued, too, by the way Monville had used curved lines to divide his interior space. Rooms in the shapes of ovals, circles, semiovals, and semicircles were disposed around a central circular stairway. "The spiral stair too was beautiful," Jefferson observed in his letter. Lit by a round skylight, the stair was hung with pots of carnations, periwinkles, heliotropes, and arum lilies, with geraniums selected from the more than eighty varieties grown in Monville's hothouses. Upstairs were bedrooms, studio, laboratory, and the library where Marie Antoinette had browsed among the volumes on gardening (figures 9, 16).

For a visit from Jefferson, or from King Gustavus of Sweden two years earlier, plans would have been brought from the little room adjoining the salon, and unrolled from between sheets of marbled paper onto the mahogany table. On display, surely, was the relief model of the Désert, built on a platform eight feet by twenty-two, as were other models Monville fabricated in his studio, where he kept a forge and a cabinetmaker's bench for that purpose. Jefferson would have been eager to see the tools of his fellow enthusiast. For the amateur creators of such gardens, plans and models had an interest rivaling that of the thing itself. In this the golden age of garden cartography, plans, drawings, and models were valued as representations of art works, that is, the follies, that were themselves representations of an architectural reality far removed by time and space. We know that among Monville's treasures were a wooden model of the Column painted to resemble stone, models of its staircase and base, clay versions of the Column with wooden bases painted in gold, wooden models of several military tents, as well as pastel drawings and two tin figures in Egyptian dress, designed to stand next to the Obelisk as the satyrs stood by the Grotto (figures 76, 93).[17]

Would Jefferson have felt at home among the busts of his compatriots George Washington and Benjamin Franklin? One wonders if Monville already owned the bust of Jefferson himself that may be among the unidentified statuary listed in the inventories of the property. If Jefferson and his companion had been shown Monville's bedroom, they would have seen Hubert Robert's painting *Le Décintrement du Pont de Neuilly* (of which there is a drawing in the Musée de Carnavalet in Paris) and works by Van Loo and Lagrénée. Here the owner's sybaritic tastes prevailed. The draperies were of hand-painted toile de Jouy, the woodwork and furniture painted dove grey, and the pure white marble mantels carved with acanthus leaves. Among the bronzes and Sèvres porcelain figures scattered on tabletops were some nudes, "in postures of which decency does not permit description."[18]

From this elevation the oval windows framed the Pyramid and Gothic ruin and, across the valley, the Little Altar and Temple of Pan. These views were reflected in the oval mirrors over the mantels. Then, as now, the vista would have embraced a panorama of treetops, not only of native sycamores, chestnuts, and lindens, but blue cedars and Virginia tulips imported from America. Perhaps Monville would have asked Jefferson's help in obtaining specimen trees, knowing that the American had obtained trees from Virginia for the garden of his friend Madame de Tessé. Hers, like the choicest specimens at the Désert de Retz, were confiscated in 1792 and placed in the former Jardin du Roi in Paris, the present Jardin des Plantes.[19]

After the viewing, what would M. de Monville have offered as refreshment? Perhaps tea in the Chinese pavilion, served from his collection of antique porcelain. If the day was hot, a servant may have rushed over from the Pyramid bearing ice for their drinks. This bit of Egyptian fantasy functioned as a working icehouse. Like the Glacier at Versailles, it was packed every winter with ice carried down from the Alps by wagon. Would other visitors have been on hand? The young queen, Marie Antoinette, who "went there several times and liked it very much"?[20] Or the writer Dorat, famous for never blotting a line, who composed some of his fables at the Désert? Or the Duc d'Orléans, soon to meet his end at the guillotine, who found it a pleasant spot to play cards?[21]

Later on, in the evening, there might have been a concert out of doors. One envisions Monville sitting down at his harp beneath the trees of the Open-Air Theater, perhaps accompanied by Maria Cosway.[22] The program may have been the one Dufort de Cheverny remembers hearing at Monville's town house, with "a piece by Rameau for several instruments" and "a concert of wind instruments, a vogue from Germany then popular at the supper parties of princes and ambassadors."[23]

In whatever manner he was entertained by M. de Monville, Jefferson relished his visit to the Désert. "The wheels of time moved on with a rapidity of which those of our carriage gave but a faint idea," he wrote to Maria Cosway afterward. "Yet in the evening when one took a retrospect of the day, what a mass of happiness we travelled over."[24]

Who was Monsieur de Monville, and how much credit should we give him for creating the Désert de Retz? To answer this question, one must sift through the memoirs of the time. For Monville has been a mysterious figure in the history of landscape art. He left us almost no papers of his own, no treatise on gardening, few letters, a very few legal documents. But he was a vigorous participant in Parisian society, a friend of many who shared his tastes for republican ideas, for things English, for the opera, for the Masonic brotherhood, and who saw in the natural garden a powerful symbol of personal liberty. It is by identifying his associates and piecing together their recollections of him that we form the following portrait of Monsieur de Monville.

Born François Nicolas Henri Racine du Jonquoy in Paris on October 4, 1734, he was descended from a family of wealthy financiers. He grew up in a house on the rue des Neuve-des-Petits-Champs belonging to his maternal grandfather, Thomas Le Monnier, the clever son of a provincial drapery merchant, who had established the family fortune in 1724 with his income as Farmer General, one of the King's forty tax-collectors. His father, Jean Baptiste Racine du Jonquoy, was Treasurer of the National Highways and Bridges before coming into the lucrative post of General Tax-Collector of Alençon. The family was related by marriage to the powerful minister the Duc de Choiseul, whose brother had married Monville's niece. As a young man, Monville himself had aspired to an ambassadorship, but had to settle for the post of Grand Master of Water and Forests for Normandy, which he assumed at the age of twenty-three.

Monville's bachelorhood was interrupted only briefly by marriage. He wed his cousin Aimable Charlotte Lucas de Boncourt in 1775, and during their marriage he used the titles Racine du Thuit, Seigneur de Monville, which he dropped later. After five years of marriage his wife died, followed a few months later by his grandfather, who left him a large income from land holdings in Normandy. Thus by the age of thirty Monville was able to relinquish his responsibilities for the forests and waterworks. He embarked on a new career as an ornament of society, for which he was superbly qualified by looks and temperament.

In an age that appreciated a gentleman's legs, Monville was celebrated for his. "One of the most handsome gentlemen in Paris," Dufort de Cheverny called him. "He was five feet eight inches tall. Built like a model, he had a fine figure, superb legs, and a slightly small but agreeable head. He was a superior dancer and was forever receiving invitations to all the balls."[25] Alas, no likeness of this paragon has come down to us. One regrets in particular the missing portrait of Monville by Madame Vigée-Lebrun. The artist lists it among the works she had completed by 1789, when she fled the country, but the painting has never turned up.[26] In its absence, we will have to rely upon the testimonies of women of taste, the pursuit of whom was one of Monville's most successful avocations.

His longest documented alliance was with Madame du Barry, the last official favorite of Louis XV. They had met in 1762, when she was an eighteen-year-old model at the fashion house of Labille. So striking was her carriage in those days, Monville enjoyed recalling later, that no matter how modestly she dressed, artists would approach her and beg to paint her nude.[27] Twenty years later, after the king had died of smallpox and Du Barry had been banished from the court, Monville remained her friend. He would drive the two miles from the Désert to her château at Louveciennes, where he was seen in the mid-1780s by the ubiquitous Vigée-Lebrun. The painter remembers the pleasures of Du Barry's hospitality, chief among them retiring after dinner to the exquisite pavilion designed for her by the young Ledoux. We can imagine Monville sitting among the guests as they sip their coffee in Ledoux's square salon, where five great windows in each wall offered a panorama of the Seine and the distant Paris skyline. To enliven his neighbor's quiet existence, Monville suggested a gardening project. In 1781 he proposed that Du Barry renovate the grounds of Louveciennes in the new English style. She agreed so readily that it alarmed the Comte d'Angivilliers, the King's Director of Building, who complained that she had "abandoned herself to this . . . grand and perhaps unwise project, in which she appears to be directed by M. de Monville." The count took it upon himself to warn Monville there would be little money in the royal budget for Du Barry's pleasure gardens.[28]

Monville had not been afraid to dally with another mistress of Louis XV, Madame d'Esparbès. The story goes that when the king complained to the lady "You have slept with all my subjects," she replied,

"Oh, sire."

"You have had the Duc de Choiseul."

"He is so strong."

"The Maréchal de Richelieu."

"He is so witty."

"Monville."

"He has such a beautiful leg."[29]

The bluestockings could be less kind. Dr. Johnson's friend Mrs. Thrale, who visited the bachelor establishment Boullée had created for Monville on the rue d'Anjou, found its atmosphere shocking. The decor made her think of "the apartments of a Roman emperor"—not a flattering comparison from the high priestess of the English Enlightenment. The Parisian saloniste Madame de Genlis, known for her musical gatherings in the rue de Bellechasse, commended Monville as a "grand suitor, young, rich, and very handsome," but "not of the court."[30]

Monville found other mistresses among the artistes of the Parisian demimonde: the actress Austrady, the singer Sophie Arnould, a star of the opera, and another opera entertainer whose lover was a M. de Craymayel, *Fermier Général*. This worthy revenged himself on his rival by placing Monville under police surveillance, leaving history a full record of Monville's romantic adventures.[31] The same Craymayel commissioned one of the masterpieces of pavilion architecture, Ledoux's 1772 Pavillon Guimard on the rue Sentier in Paris, next door to where Mozart was to reside a few years later. It was built for the dancer Marie-Madeleine Guimard, popularly known as "la Guimard," who despite her squat stature and plain face was considered the most spellbinding choreographic performer of the day. With its theater modeled on Palladio's Olympic Theater in Ve-

rona, its ceiling by David and murals by Fragonard, the Pavillon Guimard was one of the sights of Paris and so impressed Jefferson that he echoed it at the University of Virginia. We find Monville dining chez Guimard on May 4, 1778. The occasion was the marriage banquet for la Guimard's fifteen-year-old daughter. Monville had agreed to stand up for the groom.[32]

During the boom in residential building that swept Paris in the 1760s and 1770s, it was customary for owners to open their new houses to sightseers. On the evidence of the guidebooks and travel diaries, two of the most popular architectural attractions of those decades were Ledoux's pavilions for la Guimard and for Madame du Barry, known as the Temple to Terpsichore and the Temple to Love. The third was Monville's own double town house on the rue d'Anjou, now gone, which the architect Boullée had built for him in 1764. Monville's mansion and Ledoux's château at Elysée were the only private residences that Joseph, the Holy Roman Emperor, asked to see on the incognito visit he made to France in 1777 under the alias of the Comte de Falkenstein.[33] The British architect William Chambers was sufficiently interested in Monville's town house to have drawings made and sent to him in England.

The sensation caused by Ledoux's house for la Guimard moved her rival at the opera, Sophie Arnould, to insist that her lover, the architect Bélanger, build her a setting of equal distinction. The façade of the Arnould mansion does echo Ledoux's design in its stripped-down temple form and sparing use of windows. Its creator Bélanger is better known as a popularizer of the natural garden, which he traveled to England to study. He is remembered for working on both the first English garden commissioned by the royal family—the Comte d'Artois's Bagatelle of 1777—and the last of the English gardens constructed during the pre-revolutionary Paris bulding boom, in 1790 for the playwright Beaumarchais, an associate of Monville who was to play a decisive role in the fate of the Désert de Retz, as we shall see.[34]

Such were the circles Monville traveled in once he came into his inheritance. According to the historian Tilly, Monville's head was not turned by the company he kept. "He had an honest heart," Tilly writes, "and was not corrupted by the ostentation and splendor about him."[35] Although some may have disapproved of Monville's hedonism, none could dispute his talent. He played the harp well enough to accompany Jarnovitz, the greatest violinist of the day. His feats as a horseman and archer drew effusive testimonials from such sporting companions as the Prince of Nassau and the Duc d'Orléans. Bachaumont records how a great crowd gathered in the Bois de Boulogne to watch Monville bring down a pheasant with his bow and arrow.[36] Even the royal gardener Thomas Blaikie, who withheld praise from Monville as a landscape artist, concedes he was "the best archer in France and perhaps in Europe. I saw him at the chase shoot with his bow and arrow pheasant flying and many other things equally dextrous," he writes in his delightful memoir, *Diary of a Scotch Gardener at the French Court at the End of the Eighteenth Century.*[37]

As a patron, Monville acquitted himself brilliantly by the standards of today. His musical evenings featured performances by Gluck and Monsigny of selections from their latest operas. A typical dinner party chez Monville would be accompanied by seven continuous hours of music, beginning at the soup course, played by his own ensemble of six stringed instruments.[38] The musical entertainment was "the most agreeable and most fashionable imaginable," recalled his guest Dufort de Cheverny. Nothing serves Monville's latter-day reputation better than his association with the architect Boullée. Our image of him as an enlightened patron gains from the cult status of Boullée and Ledoux, whose work is thought to anticipate the twentieth-century Modern Movement. In 1764 Boullée designed two houses for Monville, one large and one small, on the rue d'Anjou near the Madeleine. Among a handful of private residences in Boullée's oeuvre, the grand Hôtel Monville can be envisioned from his comparable Hôtel Alexandre, which survives in part, as well as from drawings and engravings (figure 13).

These show an imposing two-story neoclassical town house in the configuration popularized by Mansart, that is, with a string of rooms in a U-shape around a front court entered from a narrow passage on the street.[39] The style reveals the efforts Boullée was making in the 1760s to supplant the rococo and restore dignity to the French neoclassical tradition. He used the colossal orders on both the court and garden façades, which was then unusual in domestic architecture, giving the house a surprisingly monumental air. He also replaced windows with medallions on the second story (a stage in his movement toward eliminating windows altogether). Boullée's love of windowless walls and consequent reliance on skylights expressed itself in the double-domed Turkish salon, which was lit from the top and concealed a gallery for musicians between the two domes.

The decor of this salon was exotic enough to be mentioned in guidebooks of the period. Thiéry described it as "simulating a pavilion with a view into Oriental gardens, the tree tops of which are visible between the columns which support the pavilion next to which painted nude female figures hold open the draperies."[40] The actual garden we know only from a sketchy plan, which shows a geometric layout with a single allée. Boullée's reputed disinterest in the English landscape style makes it unlikely that Monville's experiments with the irregular garden began here.

Nevertheless, Monville's taste for opulence and his weakness for secret passageways and mechanical devices are plentifully evident in his Paris houses. Dufort de Cheverny gives this swooning account of a visit to his Paris residence:

I climbed eight steps and entered a very hot stucco waiting room furnished with a magnificent stove. A valet opened and closed the double doors and I found myself in a gilded antechamber lit by a chandelier. . . . I passed into a first salon adorned with projecting columns, brilliant with concealed lights. I continued and came to a most elegant bedroom, all in crimson velvet fringed with gold. The next room was a windowless Turkish salon lined with mirrors and lit by a skylight. The doors of this enchanting retreat moved in slots conforming to the shape of the room. A secret device in the wall, when lightly pressed, opened them with marvelous expedition. I proceeded into another room and saw Monville, superbly dressed, posed writing in front of a porcelain desk. I imagined myself in a fairyland palace.[41]

With such amusements, Monville passed the decade of his thirties. At that period, there is little to prove he was more than a gifted playboy. We remember that he had not seemed serious enough to be trusted with a diplomatic post. Regarding the depth of his learning, Tilly called him "mediocre." The Scotsman Blaikie, living up to his reputation for brusqueness, dismissed him thus: "The Duc d'Orléans had many of these pretended connoisseurs about him. M. Monville was frequently of his party and a pretended connoisseur in everything."[42]

After retiring from his government post at the age of thirty, M. de Monville disappears from the public records for more than ten years. We do not hear of him again until 1774, when it is reported that he bought a farm at the village of Retz, near Chambourcy. Monville was forty when he embarked upon his garden there, no longer young by the accounting of his day. The amount of building he accomplished in the next fifteen years would indicate that in the creation of his Désert, Monville had finally found his life's work.

The site he chose was the farm and village of twelve dwellings adjacent to the king's Park of Marly and within twenty kilometers of the royal châteaux at Louveciennes, Saint-Germain-en-Laye, Versailles, and Rambouillet. With the purchase of two additional farms and some land belonging to the Abbey of Joyenval, Monville had by 1783 amassed thirty-eight hectares, an irregular parcel sloping down from the Forest of Marly toward the village. Formed like a natural amphitheater looking out toward the meadows and forests, the property encircled a central valley crossed by a brook and bounded on two sides by the Marly wall (figure 2).[43]

Through the wit of its naming and placement, Monville's garden made a pointed comment on the neighboring royal lands. Why "Désert"? The name "Le Désert" appears on maps of the adjoining countryside from that period, where it refers to an *essart*, a section of woodland that had been cleared of all its trees (figure 3). This term is compatible with the common meaning of *désert* as a "wilderness." It was the custom for the grand parks to contain a corner called a "desert" in this sense, reserved for the hermitage, philosopher's hut, or other site of contemplation and ascetic living. By calling his garden "Le Désert," Monville implies that it is such a part of the Park of Marly, and that the Park, in turn, is his. By extension, his irreverent conceit appropriates the entire complex of royal domains around him, encompassing even Versailles.

Why "Retz"? The village name is a corruption of *roi*, referring to the king's ownership, which had evolved from Roye in the twelfth century to Retz by Monville's time. It is a pose of modesty on Monville's part to adopt these humble place names, which in combination achieve a pointedly antimonarchical wit. The irony is that his garden is not a "desert" at all, but a luxurious pleasure ground; not "wild" at all, but the artful creation of a most discriminating sybarite. The implication is that it is his royal neighbors, in the unreflective enjoyment of their vast estates, who inhabit a desert.

How did Monville proceed in creating a garden on these newly acquired properties? In 1785, Georges Le Rouge published twenty-six engravings of its features, including maps, floor plans, sections, and elevations, which make up the thirteenth and largest cahier of his widely circulated *Jardins anglo-chinois à la mode*. The chief source of information on the Désert during the period of its construction, Le Rouge designates Monville as "the designer and builder of every aspect of his property." His contemporary Blaikie seems never to have doubted that Monville designed his own garden. The Scotsman probably visited the Désert during 1778–1780, while he was working on the English gardens at Bagatelle for the Comte d'Artois, the brother-in-law of Marie Antoinette. In his diary entries for this period, he calls the Désert "a garden of [Monville's] own design. He made his château in the form of an old round tower with a stair in the middle surrounded with flower pots which made a tolerable agreeable effect. . . . I cannot think but he meant to imitate the Tower of Babel."[44]

It is noteworthy that with the passage of time historians became less willing to credit the design of the Désert de Retz to an amateur such as Monville. In the twentieth century, the Désert has been attributed to architects of proven accomplishment. The most popular candidate has been Boullée, since he was employed by Monville for his Paris houses.[45] It is indeed tempting to associate the Désert with the mystique of Boullée, who is so fashionable at present. His unbuilt visionary projects reveal a sensibility that certainly would have identified with aspects of the outlandish, oversize Broken Column, namely, its apocalyptic iconography and its strategy of scaling up a single element from the classical repertoire.

The analogy with the Tower of Babel that Monville's contemporaries felt so strongly is an intriguing link to Boullée. He was haunted by the story of how God destroyed the work of these architectural overreachers and kept an illustrated copy of Kircher's treatise on the subject in his library (figure 30). Scholars believe he drew his own tower designs from the widely circulated images of the Biblical tower from seventeenth- and eighteenth-century painting.[46] Boullée created his own version of the truncated giant column in three drawings, two entitled "Lighthouse" and a third called "Circular Building" (figure 31). His surprisingly habitable interiors for huge geometrical forms are comparable to what is achieved inside the Broken Column.

But these similarities fade in the face of the obvious incompatibility of values inherent in Boullée with those of the Désert. Boullée's mechanically perfect surfaces and pure forms are hardly in the spirit of Monville's Column, with its crumbling walls and fragmentary shape. Boullée's is an idealizing architecture. His utopianism and purism put him at intellectual odds with the aesthetic of the ruin, especially one as extreme as the Broken Column, with its irreverent assertion of imperfection. The fact that Boullée was a proponent of the traditional French formal garden, although none of his rare garden designs have survived, also makes it unlikely that he would have become involved with such an enterprise as the Désert.[47]

Another of Monville's better-known contemporaries, the artist and garden designer Hubert Robert, has been credited with the conception of the garden and its follies by Cyril Connolly and Osvald Sirén, among others.[48] In 1949, Sirén introduced the Désert de Retz to twentieth-century English readers thus: "It is not generally realized in England that Hubert Robert, the great painter of Arcadian landscapes with classical ruins, was also a designer of gardens. Among the gardens that may be attributed to his inspiration is that of Méréville, (on whose walls there formerly hung some of the views of the place painted by Robert himself), Rambouillet (in part), and—the most fascinating of all—the Désert de Retz."[49] Sirén claimed that Robert designed the Pyramid, along with the garden plan, while most others associate him with the more spectacular Broken Column.

In the decades since, one has awaited documentary evidence of Robert's involvement with the Désert. But none has been discovered. This prolific artist remains a candidate solely on the strength of the visual resemblances between views at the Désert and his paintings of outdoor scenes. Sirén starts off by claiming that "no one who has visited the place and felt the charm . . . of its architectural embellishments . . . will be surprised that Hubert Robert had a part in their actual shaping." But his evidence turns out to be nothing more than the observation that, in the case of the Pyramid, "the fascinating play of brown and green against a background drenched in light is so strikingly like Hubert Robert that it must have been created, or at any rate inspired, by him."[50] The Désert's Temple of Pan does resemble Robert's painting of the Temple of Modern Philosophy at Méréville in its style and hilltop setting, but this can be explained by their common model in the Roman Temple of the Sybil at Tivoli.

Moreover, one looks in vain in Robert's landscapes for a ruin as sinister as the Broken Column. Like Boullée's purism, Robert's conception of the picturesque is too benign to accommodate the outlandishness and morbidity of the Column. The closest analog in his work is a 1783 painting of a Russian folly, a ruined tower at Tsarskoe Selo designed by Velten. It is a realistically scaled structure resembling an actual medieval fortification. As for the Désert being influenced by Robert's landscape design work, what we know of the chronology eliminates this possibility. The Désert predates his documented follies, at Méréville and Betz, at Marie Antoinette's Hamlet at Versailles, and the tomb of Rousseau at Ermenonville. Yet another candidate, the architect François Barbier, was suggested because his name was associated with drawings of the Désert from the 1780s.

Since the 1960s, however, a body of evidence has been brought to light that points back to Monville himself as designer.

It seems that Monville, following the practice for which the royal builders were notorious, was none too prompt in paying his workmen. A lawsuit settled in 1780 required Monville to pay the architecture student François Barbier a sum of 6,000 pounds, money owing him for work on the Désert.[51] In the records of these proceedings, this long-ago dispute over artistic credit has come to life. The reader is invited to imagine the "remarkable confrontations that must have taken place before the presiding official, with M. de Monville and Barbier each appearing with his portfolio of designs in search of paternity."[52]

Thanks to this lawsuit, we have detailed knowledge of how specific follies were designed. The usual procedure was for Monville to make sketches that Barbier rendered into finished drawings or clay models, although in some instances, Barbier's model came first. The records of the suit designate Monville as the originator of the concepts for the Temple of Pan and the Chinese House, as well as two follies never executed, including a Siamese tent and a rustic pavilion. Barbier is credited with the original designs for the Temple of Repose, an obelisk of painted tin, and some greenhouses. Barbier was awarded another 1,500 pounds for his work on the construction of the Pyramid and enlargement of the Chinese House, where his duties included negotiating with the builders. His subordinate role is indicated by his title, "designer" rather than "architect." There is no mention of Barbier in connection with the most imaginative folly, the Broken Column, which was built in 1781, after the suit was settled.

Recently, even more emphatic claims on Monville's behalf have come from Sweden, where the only original drawings of the Désert from the time of its construction have been preserved, thanks to Gustavus III.[53] Monville sent the king these drawings after the latter's visit to the Désert in 1784, receiving in return the gift of a diamond-studded gold box. These unsigned, pen-and-wash folio drawings were known for decades only as the "Stockholm drawings," since the Swedish owners did not realize what they depicted. The most unusual is a phantasmagoric panorama showing the Broken Column, Little Altar, and Temple of Pan that has been attributed to Carmontelle. It is unlike any of the images in Le Rouge or elsewhere. The others form a series, apparently in a single hand, showing elevations and sections of the Chinese House and Broken Column and floor plans of the Column, all closely resembling the engravings Le Rouge published in July of 1785 (figures 4–12).

The set had been broken up during Gustavus's lifetime and individual drawings later found their way into three different Swedish institutions. The Column elevation ended up in the National Museum in Stockholm, where it was attributed to Monville's assistant the architect François Barbier, while its floor plans were misfiled in the Royal Library as "a project for a ruined column in the garden of Rosersberg." Osvald Sirén was the first to find and make use of the complete set of drawings. In 1949, Sirén pronounced them "historically and aesthetically the most valuable documents that have come down to us pertaining to the Désert de Retz," a view Magnus seconded when he called the Le Rouge depictions "naive" by comparison.[54]

One sympathizes with the Swedish scholars' eagerness to make claims for their treasure. Who would not be moved by the history of these exquisite long-lost drawings and the romance of their association with the doomed King Gustavus, amateur dramatist, alchemist, and architect, whose assassination at a masked ball furnished the plot for Verdi's opera *Un Ballo in Maschera*? The vision of the Désert presented here is indeed enchanting. The pale color washes and delicacy of line impart an atmosphere to the Chinese House that evokes the subtle hues of its actual stained wood exterior and the refinement of its Louis XVI interior. But there is no reason we must accept Sirén's assessment of the drawings' value because they contain, as he puts it, "details which are missing in Le Rouge's engravings."

Correspondence in the Swedish archives establishes that all of the drawings except the Carmontelle view had to have been executed between the time of the king's visit on July 14, 1784, and March 28, 1785, when a packet was sent from Monville by the Swedish ambassador in Paris. This chronology admits the possibility that the Stockholm drawings were copied from the engravings, or from the drawings from which the engravings were done, which must have been finished by March 1785 for a publication appearing that July. For the "missing" details are not architectural, but are embellishments such as bouquets of flowers, paintings on the walls, and the figures with parasols in Chinese dress, all of which could have been added to the basic images in Le Rouge's engravings by an inspired artist.

Among the correspondence is a rare surviving letter of Monville's. This graceful missive presents the drawings to Gustavus and recalls their meeting at the Désert de Retz. It is primarily on the basis of this letter that the National Swedish Art Museums decided in 1986 that the drawings are in Monville's own hand.[55] Here again, one would like nothing better than to agree. But Monville's wording, which does not specify who executed the drawings, makes the letter insufficient proof in itself. The dates of the correspondence, however, establishing 1784 and 1785 as the period when the drawings would have had to have been made, are important in that they cancel out the case for Barbier, whose work at the Désert was concluded by 1780.

Original drawings by Gutavus do survive, telling us that upon receiving Monville's packet, the king drew a scheme for a round domed building very like the Column in plan, and another showing an octagonal palace at Haga. He gave the latter to the architects of a 1786 plan for Haga in which oval rooms are disposed around a circular core. Being octagonal, Gustavus's plan does not resemble the Column House as closely as Jefferson's rotunda. At Haga, clusters of rooms in the corners repeat the Column's basic configuration of two large ovals linked at the top by a smaller semioval.[56] It is likely that Gustavus lent Monville's originals to his architects soon after receiving them. Designs by Louis Jean Desprez for towers and a Chinese pavillion show the influence of the Désert. The Stockholm drawings of the Chinese House were given to the Royal Library by the estate of the great Swedish garden designer Fredrick Magnus Piper. It would explain the mystery of the drawings' disappearance and dispersal if they had been given over for study to such artists in the king's employ.[57]

If it is unlikely that Boullée, Robert, or Barbier could have designed the Désert de Retz, why should we not reconsider Monville? If he did design his garden himself, what would have been his reasons for doing so? Why would this worldling, who had spent his entire life in Paris, devote his last years to creating a country retreat, in a place with no connection to his boyhood or family history? It is perhaps wisest to refrain from biographical speculation on this point, and to assume that, once again, Monville was following fashion. In 1774, Monville would have been nowise more the man of the world than in his retirement from it.

The last half of the eighteenth century had witnessed a change in the country pleasures of the aristocracy, as the vogue of rusticity replaced the ritualized entertainments of the grand châteaux. Monville's Désert partook of the cultural ethos, codified in Rousseau's *Julie; ou, La Nouvelle Héloïse*, that made it a mark of refinement for ladies and gentlemen to seek shelter in peasant huts, sustenance in picnic lunches, and amusement in the study of botany.

The appropriate settings for such pastimes were not the geometric gardens glorified under the reign of Louis XIV, whose atmosphere the new generation found "sad," but those where, in the words of Diderot's dictum, "nature was everywhere apparent." Enthusiasts of the antiformalist garden sought cultural justification in the mystiques of England and China, and aesthetic guidance in painting and literature. These disciplines were the sources of themes for outdoor picture making (thus the term "picturesque garden") and story telling. The gardening enterprise aimed at an ambitious form of emotion management. Views were created resembling paintings or recalling events from myth or literature with the aim of producing desired states of feeling in the observer.

Among the overlapping tendencies within this movement was the awkwardly termed *"jardin anglo-chinois,"* as Le Rouge entitled fifteen publications in his twenty-one-volume series. It owed its English origin to the historic revolt against formal landscaping in the 1730s, when William Kent "leapt the wall and saw all nature was a garden." The work of English innovators such as Kent, Bridgeman, and Whately was well known in France from the mid-century onward, as was the considerable body of literature promoting the new style, from Sir William Temple's *Gardens of Epicurus* to the writings of Alexander Pope and Addison's *Spectator*. Visits to England by Voltaire, Montesquieu, and Rousseau had converted them to partisans of its garden revolutions. The Marquis de Girardin studied English models firsthand before embarking on his elaborate folly garden at Ermenonville. He synthesized their lessons in *De la composition des paysages*, his widely read treatise on applying English gardening principles to French conditions. The royal gardener Bélanger made at least two tours, during which he sketched buildings at Stowe and Stourhead and the rockery and cascades of Leasowes and Dovedale.

We do not know if Monville, too, visited England. If not, he could have found sufficient models in Prince Stanislaus's much-visited rococo garden begun at Lunéville in 1747, with its Chinese and Turkish follies; Watelet's rustic folly garden at Moulin-Joli (1751); or Girardin's eclectic Ermenonville, the most elaborate of the French picturesque gardens (1762). All were early examples of the French antiformalist garden whose construction predated the Désert.

The closest resemblances exist between features of the Désert and those of roughly contemporaneous gardens, such as the Duc de Chartres's Monceau, designed by Carmontelle beginning in 1773; Cassan, built in the 1770s or 1780s, possibly with the help of Fragonard; and Chantilly, begun in 1775. Later came Jean-Joseph de Laborde's Méréville, begun in 1784; Betz, 1780; and Rambouillet in 1783, all executed under the influence of Hubert Robert.

These estates bear the stamp of the intellectual milieu to which Monville undoubtedly belonged. It was made up of aristocratic landowners, architects, horticulturists, philosophers, and painters who in the third quarter of the century took up garden building with a fervor that William Howard Adams has called hysterical in its intensity. Their collective achievement in just two decades far outstrips the pace of the more celebrated English garden builders of the century. The results are best understood in contemporary terms as artistic collaborations, in which ideas are difficult to attribute to individuals, where artists are continually replacing each other on the same project, and where the final product is more similar to an evolving multimedia theatrical event than a finished architectural statement.

Establishing a simple lineage for the Désert is made difficult, also, by the fact that after the first flurry of exchange between England and France the *jardin anglais* became overlaid with a tangle of other purported influences. The ambivalence of French Anglomanes made them loathe to name the English as sole inventors of the natural garden, preferring to give credit to the ancients or to the genius of the Chinese. The Chinese alternative was given credence by the writings of a onetime employee of the Dutch East India Company, William Chambers, whose 1757 *Design of Chinese Buildings* was the spark that ignited an existing China mania. Although the accuracy of his purportedly firsthand descriptions was later questioned, Chambers's interpretation of a Chinese aesthetic seemed confirmed at the time by returning French Jesuit missionaries, by drawings and engravings, and, very quickly, by the popularity of European building in a "Chinese" vein, of which influential early examples at Kew Gardens outside London were designed by Chambers himself.

By the 1770s, also, notions of the picturesque taken from the English countryside at mid-century were being influenced by the Italian landscape, as observed by the painters Hubert Robert and Fragonard on their journeys south after 1750, and depicted in a tradition that embraced Watteau, Poussin, Boucher, Salvator Rosa, and Claude Lorrain. As a feature in the landscape, the emotionally charged image of the ruin from antiquity, half overgrown and surrounded by scenes of teeming contemporary life, had been made a cultural icon by Piranesi's scenes of Rome. Into this thicket of rich, rebounding, and sometimes sham influences stepped M. de Monville in 1774.

What specific models might he have used for his follies? In the Chinese vein, he surely would have known Chambers's widely circulated images of the Pagoda and House of Confucius he designed at Kew (figure 28), published in his *Gardens of Kew* in 1763, and the architect Emmanuel Here's engravings of the Kiosk and Chinese Building at Lunéville, published in 1753 and 1756. Of actual oriental buildings near Paris, he would have known Chanteloup. The Chinese Pavilion at Cassan, which still exists, was likely to have been built after 1778, too late to have influenced Monville's Chinese House, which leaves him relying primarily on drawings for inspiration.

Although ingeniously designed and crafted, the Chinese House at Retz demonstrates the undeniable superficiality of the "Chinese" character of much of the European oriental architecture of the period. We must agree with Osvald Sirén, who examined it in the 1940s, when it was still intact, that this is "a structure that is essentially French." Sirén observed that its "Chinoiserie is contained largely in the decoration, in the carved and painted ornaments of the façades, the vase-shaped chimneys, and the crowning railing of the balustrade on top of the lantern. It is evident that the designer of the Maison Chinoise had no real Chinese models or other sources to refer to, but only ornamental drawings, such as he copied to the best of his ability on the high door panels and rather more freely in the bamboo pillars and their brackets" (figures 10–12, 18, 38, 47).[58]

Monville's Temple of Pan, on the other hand, closely follows the convention from antiquity of setting a circular temple on a commanding hilltop, as do similar follies at Stowe, Méréville, and Ermenonville. Its form as a ruin is taken from Temple of the Sibyl at Tivoli, where the front row of columns stands while the back crumbles away (figure 20). Monville could have copied this configuration from one of the numerous paintings of the site by such artists as Claude and Boucher, or from the Marquis de Girardin's Temple of Modern Philosophy at Ermenonville, which had been built in the 1760s in explicit imitation of the real Tivoli ruin. The Ermenonville temple's strongest resemblance is to two paintings by Hubert Robert, one of the ancient site at Tivoli and one of the Temple of Love at Méréville, which Robert himself designed in the 1780s, after the completion of the Désert de Retz. These resemblances are marked enough to suggest that the follies at both Ermenonville and at Méréville were Robert's designs, and to raise again the possibility of Robert's influence on Monville (figures 21–23).

The model for Monville's Pyramid was a Roman building equally well known at the time, the mausoleum of Caius Cestius on the Appian Way. This monument was a favorite of painters and was the subject of a series of Piranesi engravings that we know to have been in Monville's possession at the time of his death.[59] We see its four-sided form repeatedly in the funerary architecture of the picturesque gardens, including the pyramid tomb still standing in the Parc Monceau in Paris (figures 24–27).

Suffice it to say that there was a wealth of precedent, with varied and sometimes contradictory cultural meanings, for Monville to draw upon for the architecture of the Désert, the Broken Column excepted. His farm and thatched-roof cottage belong to the rustic vernacular of Moulin-Joli, the Cottage and Dairy at Rambouillet, the Hamlet at Versailles, and their numerous equivalents elsewhere. The rustic bridge has close counterparts in drawings of Ermenonville. The pyramid and obelisk, part of the heritage of world architecture, were represented at Lunéville, Monceau, and Méréville. Like these gardens, the Désert had its tomb. The Tartar Tent is in the more playful spirit of Lunéville, where the owner, the exiled Polish king, Stanislaus, imported the Eastern European taste for flimsy, tent-like garden structures. The tradition flourished in the painted tent of Bagatelle, now gone, and the magnificent tent standing at Drottningholm in Sweden.

In the 1980s a group of prominent scholars launched the intriguing hypothesis that Monville's program was dictated by Masonic ritual. At the close of this golden age of Freemasonry, aristocrats of Monville's artistic and freethinking disposition were likely to be members of the secret brotherhood, as was his intimate friend and fellow garden creator the Duc d'Orléans. Although Monville's name is not listed on the rolls of Paris Freemasons, his friend the duke was not only its grand master but installed his own Masonic lodge in the Pavillon at his Parc Monceau, built one year before Monville began construction of the Désert.[60] This Masonic folly was connected by a passageway to the Winter Garden, which housed a secret grotto used for initiation rites. This chronology, as well as the friendship between the two, has fueled speculation that the Désert, too, was intended for Masonic purposes.

The visitor to the Désert de Retz enters through what is its most primitive structure architecturally, a grotto of jagged rocks. This fact has been interpreted by William Howard Adams as evidence that Monville's follies were ordered to guide the Masonic initiate upward through the history of civilization, passing from the primitive grotto to the sublime temple.[61] Olausson takes us on a Masonic walk through the Désert, where we imagine the initiate's attention directed first to the Grotto, then to the Pyramid, and then to the Broken Column. Could the Désert have also been a set for Masonic opera? Much has been made of the fact that Mozart's Masonic opera *The Magic Flute,* which is contemporaneous with the Parc Monceau and the Désert, features a grotto and temple in the 1791 staging of the second act. The Désert would certainly have made a striking setting for such a musical enterprise. Its Open-Air Theater, a simple stone platform with elm trees as the backdrop, has been praised as natural compared to such outdoor theaters as the one at Ermenonville, where painted backdrops of pastoral scenes were set up. If one stands back from Monville's theater, however, one realizes that the audience would also have been looking straight at the Broken Column, rising above the elms. The Broken Column, a symbol on the Mason's apron, may well have been the intended backdrop to performances there.

It is intriguing to be reminded that images of the classical temple, pyramid, grotto, and the shattered column were common in the iconography of late eighteenth-century Freemasonry. It is even more tantalizing to imagine, as Olausson does, that the two workshops at the Désert were intended for alchemy, not model making. Were the forge and chemicals found by the revolutionary officials used for Monville's experiments with the philosopher's stone? Olausson thinks so, knowing that alchemy was practiced only twelve miles away, at the Parc Monceau, where Monville's friend the duke was trying to turn the bones of Pascal into gold.[62]

There were Masonic gardens, built as such in Monville's time, primarily in Germany.[63] But one hesitates to conclude that his was one of them. One reason is that the follies central to a Masonic reading of the Désert, the Grotto Entry and Broken Column, were constructed late, in the 1780s. It appears that work on the Désert was begun without the guidance of a general plan, which is surprising if the garden were to carry forth a ritualistic program. No plan from before 1785 has been found, but one would have been of limited usefulness, since the shape of the property changed significantly in the first twelve years with purchases and exchanges. The Le Rouge plan is more likely to be a record of work completed by that date than to reflect an earlier conception. Singleness of purpose is not characteristic of the design process we associate with the habits of Monville, who created elaborate schemes only to modify or abandon them.

The strongest case against the Masonic hypothesis, however, is not found in historical documents, or argued from their absence, as with Monville's name on the rolls of the Paris Freemasons. The evidence exists in the physical form of the garden, which one can see just as well today as in Monville's time. A small open valley, where nothing is hidden, the site is not conducive to a ritual progression where the initiate views only one scene at a time. Nor does the architecture of the follies cater to the society's need for secrecy. At Monceau, rituals were held in an enclosed, dimly lit grotto that could be entered only through a secret door in an obscure corner of a hothouse. Music for the proceedings was wafted in from unseen players stationed in a room above. Monville's Paris house, with its concealed doors and piped-in music, is evidence that he, too, could delight in the hidden. But we find no evidence of such appointments in the structures at the Désert. Monville seems too much of a creative individualist to have been interested in carrying out an institutional regime. His Désert resists reduction to a thematic program, although it plays brilliantly on the themes of the age.

What so moves visitors about this garden is its powerful sense of place, as one says today. Its enchanting secret-garden atmosphere is best understood as a triumph of form, an effect of the overall handling of proportion and detail. Although Monville's architectural creations could hardly be more artificial, his landscaping is natural in its effects. One could even call it modest. Here is landscape art achieved without engineering heroics, the earth moving and river diverting employed by the Marquis de Girardin, for example. Nor is it dependent on visual tricks: there are no forced perspectives, no paths concealed as ha-has, no buildings screened with shrubs, masquerading as woods. The harmonious atmosphere of the valley is not disturbed by the presence of twenty follies, an accomplishment that should have surprised Monville's English colleagues, who found French picturesque gardens repellently overdecorated and cluttered, with too many follies too close together.

The Désert is tiny in area for such a garden and Monville wisely gave it just one architectural focus, the Broken Column. His restraint won him compliments at the time from the Prince de Ligne, who reports, "There is but one temple, dominating a simple ravine against the wood, visible from every point on the property, to which it adds a highly decorative note." Although visually outlandish, the Column is in scale with the piece of countryside it occupies.[64]

So exotic is the Column as an example of representational architecture, a mock ruin, that it has diverted attention from the other formal achievements at the Désert. The ingenuity of the Column floor plan, which solves the problem of dividing the circle, has been given its due. It takes to the level of tour de force the vogue for curved-walled rooms, disposing fifteen round, oval, semicircular, and semioval rooms around a circular stair, without wasting the remaining shell-shaped spaces.

The Column exterior is a design victory of greater order, moreover, one that has not been acknowledged. Monville's choice of a round building as his main house solved a problem that had plagued the French ever since they began adding English gardens to their existing estates: How to join an asymmetrical garden, with curving paths and undulating topography, to a château and outbuildings that were rectangular or square? How to fit the square peg of the French château into the round hole of the English garden? The border area between house and garden was rarely handled successfully. In the opinion of the Scottish gardener Blaikie, the failure to integrate architecture and garden design was the damning flaw of the French.

This failure can be explained by the incompatibility of the concurrent revolutions in architecture and in garden design. The garden revolution of the mid-eighteenth century banished right angles and the straight line. But its chronological and ideological counterpart in architecture, the movement misnamed "Louis XVI," banished the curves of the rococo. There was no new architecture that shared the landscape revolution's association of political freedom with the curved line. Monville solves this problem that confounded his contemporaries. He invents his own genre of architecture to fit his irregular landscape, first by making the château itself round.

In the plan of his garden, the system of pathways connecting the follies is described as a labyrinth by Blaikie, and so it appears in the map published in Le Rouge. The Désert would appear to lack the traditional promenade that leads the viewer from scene to scene. This formal circuit did exist, however. It was inside the Column, where the viewer walked in a circle from window to window taking in the views. The novelty of the columnar château provided the opportunity for the novelty of an interior circuit, with the entire building functioning as a viewing device.

By the scale and placement of his round château, Monville enhances the natural topography of his site. He sets down his tower at the highest point of the undulating valley, where it appears to grow up like a tree trunk from the top of a hill. Seeing the Column as a tree reminds us that it is an explicit reference not only to the Doric and Tuscan models but to the primitive architecture that fascinated Monville's age. Writers such as the Abbé Laugier had popularized the concept of man's first house, "the model from which all the magnificences of architecture have been imagined." Drawings of the so-called "primitive hut" as a leaf-roofed structure supported by tree trunks were widely circulated and influenced a genre of rustic garden structures using unpeeled logs. According to this concept, the classical column evolved from the tree trunk, an analogy rendered literal in the Broken Column. This folly has the Romantic strangeness of a hybrid, a creation half organic and half man-made, both a shaped and fluted column base and a tree stump with a barklike surface and leaves sprouting from its top.

The conceit of the Column as the fragment of a great temple, nearly 400 feet high, gives a second level of scale to the site, in which the valley is dwarfed by the ghost of a gargantuan structure. In this way, the eighteenth-century cult of the colossal is honored in the aesthetic of the Désert, though in imagination only. The sight of the fragment generates a second, superhuman dimension in the mind of the viewer. A corollary response is the realization that giants are at hand. Coming upon the Column, a human visitor feels the fear of the fairy tale hero stumbling up against the giant's boot.

For the viewer who identifies with the giants, on the other hand, or with the Old Testament God who struck down the Tower of Babel, the conceit of the colossal temple is exhilarating. In our unbelieving age, it is easier to respond to the purely spatial implications of the imaginary realm. According to the Doric formula, height equals eight times the diameter, the full-scale column would stand at 384 feet. The architectural footprint of such a temple would extend beyond the borders of

the garden. Its encroachment onto neighboring property is another of Monville's appropriation strategies, an aggressive gesture by which he plants his flag in territory he does not own. The originality of this garden is in its tinkerings with scale, with the resulting implications about ownership and power.

Monville's pastoral experiment did not survive the Revolution. By 1788 we find him trying to sell his townhouse to the Swedish ambassador, who decided on the Hôtel de Salm instead. In preparation for leaving the country in 1790, he offered both the Désert and his city house to his friend Beaumarchais, who refused him the asking price of 400,000 pounds. That year the playwright built a new house near the Bastille, using stone from its recent demolition, with interiors by Hubert Robert and an English garden by Bélanger. Monville, who would have been informed of shifts in the political weather through his contacts at the Palais Royal, did not sell the Désert until the last possible moment. On July 21, 1792, he accepted 108,000 pounds from an English buyer, Lewis Disney Ffytche. The next day, the political atmosphere darkened with the invasion of the Duke of Brunswick. As the property of a foreigner, the Désert was immediately appropriated by the revolutionaries, who stripped the houses of their furnishings and dug up the valuable plants and trees. But Monville was legally free of the place, and had arranged to be paid in convertible currency.[65]

The only durable evidence of Monville's passage on this earth is what remains of the Désert de Retz. His fabulous house by Boullée is gone, the victim of clearing for the Boulevard Malesherbes in the nineteenth century. It is curious that a man with his aesthetic drive left no literary legacy. Monville is an anomaly among the owners of picturesque gardens in that he did not glorify his enterprise in a treatise on garden theory. He left us no equivalent of Watelet's *Essai sur les jardins*, the Prince de Ligne's *Un Coup d'oeil sur beloeil*, the Marquis de Girardin's *De la composition des paysages*, Morel's *Théorie des jardins*, or the

Duc d'Harcourt's *Traité de la décoration des dehors des jardins et des parcs*.

How did Monville survive the Revolution? Although he divested himself of his properties by 1792, he did not emigrate after all, but remained in Paris, in quarters on the rue de Clichy. There, according to the historian Tilly, "he was misguided enough to remain a friend of the Duc d'Orléans when his society had become an embarrassment."[66] Why Monville remained loyal to this treacherous member of the royal family is one of the riddles of his character. One hypothesis is that they were tied by the bonds of Freemasonry. Those who argue that Monville was a Freemason point out that the future Philippe Egalité, as Grand Master of the Paris Freemasons, was likely to have recruited his friend. In the opinion of Tilly, Monville was innocent of knowledge of his friend's political "crimes" but "persisted in the attachment out of weakness, perhaps believing that the duke could protect him from danger."[67] Could Monville have so misjudged the temper of the revolutionaries? When he was summoned for trial by the Revolutionary Tribunal, the chief charge made against him was "associating with the infamous Duc d'Orléans." Monville's "sybaritisme" was cited as well, specifically his "keeping 'la petite Sarah,' an actress at Montansier."[68] Monville pleaded illness. Instead of being imprisoned in the Conciergerie, as the summons specified, he was kept under arrest at home, and later at a house of detention in Paris. Before he could be tried, the Terror ended. Monville was freed. His survival earned him the compliments of Tilly, who called him a man who "had found the trick of getting through the Revolution, to die in his own bed."[69] Had he been younger, the flamboyant Monville might have lived to become one of the Revolution's legendary survivors, along with Lafayette and Talleyrand. As it was, old age carried him off within five years of the execution of his friend the Duc d'Orléans. After a life spent "giving himself to all the girls, a different one each night, he passed his last six years with a young showgirl. . . . He had spent his last sou and left nothing but debts."[70]

After Monville's death, his garden rested in government hands until 1811. It is to the confiscation of the Désert that we owe our most reliable knowledge of it. The records of the repeated seizures, inventories, and sales of the property under the Republic and the Empire between 1793 and 1817 have left us a detailed catalog of the contents of the grounds and buildings.[71] These documents are our instrument for penetrating the mystique that has attached itself to Monville's garden and for reconciling the differing descriptions of the place left us by artists and writers.

Some of these have been so poetic as to encourage a skeptical view of their literal truth. When Le Rouge included a pair of torch-bearing satyrs in his view of the entrance to the garden, for example, one assumed that the artist had been carried away by his imagination. How chastening it is, therefore, to know that government inventories of 1794 list "a pair of satyrs" among the effects found in a closet on Monville's property. One hopes the recording scribe was equally edified.

From these records, we can have the following picture of the garden and its follies as it was in its final state in about 1790.

Constructed around 1781, the Broken Column was of stone, fifty feet in diameter and fifty-five feet high, with five stories, one underground. The alternating rhythm of bays gave the exterior the fluting of a classical column, especially when the windows were obscured by light-colored shades, drawn from the inside. The windows of the first three stories were rectangular, square, and oval respectively, while the fourth story was illuminated by hidden windows and a skylight. The kitchens were not in the basement, as shown in the cross-section published by Le Rouge, which is of doubtful accuracy. The basement was connected by a tunnel to kitchens in the cottage next door.

Each of the upper stories had four main rooms disposed around the central spiral stair. On the first floor, two large oval rooms served as salon and dining room. Two smaller, semioval rooms were a bedroom and an entry. Between their curving walls were four semicircular spaces used as coat closet, toilet, and offices. The remaining area was divided into closets and passageways so that no space was wasted. The second story was arranged much the same as the third. On the third, the distinguishing theme was the repetition of ovals, the oval windows echoed by the mirrors over the mantels. On the top floor were a servant's room, a storage room for furniture, and the grand studio, connected to the laboratory below by a private stairway.

The laboratory and studio were fitted out for model-making with a forge, anvil, easel, and carpenter's workbench. The public rooms were paneled or in sculpted wood painted dove gray to match the furniture. Walls were covered with hand-painted or printed linen, some in Indian patterns, or plain toile de Jouy. Mirrors were placed to reflect views of the garden. Sconces in the shape of pinecones were of gilded bronze, copper, and gold alloy. All the mantels were white, carved with acanthus leaves. Along the edge of the spiral stairs were hung clay pots holding a changing display of flowers from the hothouse: geraniums, heliotropes, arum lilies, carnations, and periwinkles.

Set in a terraced garden on the edge of a lake, the two-story Chinese House was constructed around 1777 from a type of Indian teak used in shipbuilding. The façade was made up of panels of carving and latticework, trimmed with violet and red paint, and divided by columns carved to imitate bamboo. The three-tiered roof was covered in fish-scale tiles and topped by a lantern and latticework railing. The roofs curved down to extended eaves, with bells hanging from the corners. Vase-shaped chimneys sat on the lower roofs. On the ground floor was a salon, an antechamber with a ceramic fireplace, and a office outfitted with a warming pan for food. The second story was

taken up by a library, linked to the salon by a secret stairway. The library was paneled in mahogany in Louis XVI style, the walls covered with white flowered paper and hung with Chinese silk, and was furnished with divans recessed into alcoves. The bed was of beechwood, with coverings of bleached cotton trimmed in toile de Jouy printed with a Persian design.

The Désert included among its other follies the Temple of Pan, a free-standing Doric peristyle of plastered brick, which had a row of columns that extended around the front only, exposing an unfinished boxlike back. Inside, a semicircular anteroom led to a square room. The Icehouse Pyramid was a four-sided stone pyramid set on a square base, designed after the Roman pyramid of Caius Cestius on the Appian Way. An arched doorway in the center led downward into the cavity used to store ice. The edges were outlined with rusticated stonework, and urns sat at the four corners. At the Temple of Repose, a carved wooden door was flanked by two pair of rusticated columns. The Ruined Gothic Church included the walls and arched window with tracery fragment from an actual thirteenth-century church, from the village of Retz. The Grotto Entry was a doorway in the stone wall framed by protruding plaster rocks, supporting two tin satyrs holding torches. The Little Altar, a stone column decorated with garlands, served as the base for a tipped urn. The Open-Air Theater was a stone platform with a carved panel extending along the front and with garlands at each end, flanked with two urns in the Louis XVI style. A four-sided tent in the military style made of painted tin, the Tartar Tent was set on the Island of Happiness in the north lake. The Obelisk, also cut from tin, was painted to imitate stone. The Tomb was a horizontal stone structure in the shape of a truncated pyramid, decorated with a carved stone panel in front, and the Outbuilding was a thatched-roof cottage with walls painted Pompeian red. There is no detailed description of the Orangerie, Hermitage, Hothouses, Dairy, Model Farm, or Cottage, although their existence is documented in Le Rouge and elsewhere.

What became of the Désert after the Revolution? The government did not hesitate to sell off the valuable furnishings and plants, but was uncertain how to use the property itself, designated an "objet de luxe" by the revolutionary bureaucracy. In 1806 the land was returned to the Englishman who had bought it from Monville, Lewis Disney Ffytche, only to be repossessed by the government in 1811 and sold to one Lébigre, who paid by cutting the trees for lumber.[72] Ffytche regained his property in 1816, after settling the claims of Monville's creditors, and his heirs sold it in 1827. From 1843 to 1853, it was in the hands of the Scribe family, who deserves credit for taking the first photographs of the follies. These early photos serve to confirm the existence of some of the more romantic details in the engravings from the previous century, notably the cracks and jagged roof of the Broken Column in the 1850 photograph (figure 37).

In 1856, the Désert was bought by the economist Frédéric Passy, later a winner of the Nobel Peace Prize, who replanted the original pattern of forest land, oak groves, and meadow. The park as we know it dates from the nineteenth century, although individual trees from Monville's time have survived. Passy also renovated the Column, replacing the skylight with a conventional roof and evening out the broken roofline. Photographs from the turn of the century show the Passy family living in the Broken Column and operating the farm. In 1912 a delegation of scholars reported that the follies were still in good condition, including the Grotto Entry and the Chinese House. Panoramic photographs from that era indicate the location of the follies and plantings, and show sheep grazing in the meadow in front of the Column House.[73]

It was after its next sale, to the local landowner Georges Courtois in 1936, that the garden slid into a state of decay that aroused the concern of preservationists, among them the architect Jean-Charles Moreux, who published the first full modern-day account of the garden in 1938, documented by photographs by Raymond Lécuyer.[74] With the support of the writers Colette and Jacques Prévert, Moreux succeeded in having the property classified as a historic monument in 1939. This formality, however, did not induce the Courtois family to take steps to protect their property.

Disused and unguarded since the thirties, the follies were nevertheless still standing as late as 1948. During this period it was precisely its ruined condition that attracted to the Désert the artists and photographers who provide a record of its gradual decay. The evocative 1938 Lécuyer photos show the Chinese House with its chimneys, wood panels, and tiles intact, but sagging slightly at one end. The plaster rocks have crumbled away from the entry in the Marly wall. The Chinese House is still there in the late forties, when Osvald Sirén took a series of exquisite photos of the Désert. But by 1953, Colette was lamenting that "one wing of the Chinese edifice has just fallen, the rest is crumbling. . . . Is intervention indicated? If so it better be soon."[75]

In 1960 a nineteen-year-old architecture student at the Ecole des Beaux-Arts in Paris, Olivier Choppin de Janvry, discovered the Désert and took it up as the subject of his dissertation. Now an architect with a specialty in restoration, who has renovated the Chinese Pavilion at Cassan and other historic sites, Choppin de Janvry has made saving the Désert his life's avocation. During the early 1960s, he joined the group of intellectuals who urged the Minister of Culture to take steps to save the Désert. By 1966, André Malraux, then the Minister of Culture, instituted a new law under his name that gave the government the power to repair historic buildings and demand the cooperation of their legal owners. Although Malraux himself singled out the Désert as a case requiring immediate attention, the law was not applied there until 1973, when Choppin de Janvry was appointed to begin a program of emergency repairs.

The application of the Malraux law did not prevent the collapse of the Chinese House, which vanished into the lake in 1972, or provide security to prevent the theft of the paneling and mantels from the Column House. In 1983, Choppin de Janvry and a fellow enthusiast, Paris banker Jean-Marc Heftler, bought a controlling interest in the property for a token sum from its new owner, M. M. Worms and Company. They formed the Société Civile du Désert de Retz to embark on a restoration of the site, with approximately half of the costs paid by the Ministry of Culture and the rest from private sources.[76]

Since 1988, the Pyramid has been restored and the exterior of the Broken Column has been resurfaced and returned to its original appearance as a ruin, with the cracks and jagged top looking uncannily as they do in the eighteenth-century images. The Tartar Tent has been reconstructed out of a contemporary metal alloy, painted blue and gold as was the original. Plans are underway for restoration of the Gothic Church, the Commons, the Temple of Pan, and the Chinese House, enough of whose roof tiles and painted and carved timbers were salvaged that the decorative detail can be recaptured. It was decided not to restore the interior of the Broken Column to its original intricate configuration. The spiral stairway and windows have been reproduced, but the floors are open lofts that presently house the full-time restoration workers.

The most awesome change brought by restoration is the opening up of the perspectives across the meadow toward the Broken Column and the Temple of Pan. As recently as 1988, the central meadow was still the wilderness beloved by Colette, where volunteer maples and ash had engulfed the groves of oak set out by Monville. Out of this jungle, the harmonious vistas in the engravings of Laborde have snapped back into place.[77] By 1990 the meadow had been reseeded with grass, the creek restored, the lakes cleaned, and 120 historic and specimen trees rehabilitated. The boxwood walls of the Temple of Repose have taken root, while behind the Column, the kitchen garden has been re-created with fruit trees and vegetables tended by resident gardeners.[78]

The restoration of the Désert de Retz has not been implemented without controversy. The arrangement made with its 1983 owner, M. M. Worms and Company, allowed for a golf course designed by Robert Trent-Jones to occupy agricultural land belonging to the garden along the Saint-Germain border, about 375 acres or a third of the original property, as a buffer against more intensive development. The rationale was that this area's original function as a pastoral backdrop to the views from the follies would be fulfilled as well by a golf course as by farmland. Once the landscaping for the course was underway, however, the Société judged that the terrain was being changed more radically than the permits allowed and obtained a court order that stopped construction in 1990–1991. As of this writing, the future of Le Golf Joyenval is still in dispute.[79]

The late 1980s brought media celebrity to this forgotten garden. It was the site of a televised press conference by President Mittérrand, its owners the recipients of awards and grants. Visitors are admitted one day a month during the summer, and the Société intends to use the Column as a study center similar to Dumbarton Oaks in Washington, D.C. once the restoration is completed.[80]

It was nearly too late to prevent the Désert de Retz from going the way of France's other eighteenth-century picturesque gardens. Its last-minute rescue is a symptom of the sudden renewal of appreciation for this most ambitious yet ephemeral art. It is perhaps in compensation for the loss of so much of our environmental heritage that garden restoration has been taken up by the generation that witnessed the destruction of the market of Les Halles in Paris.

The restoration of M. de Monville's Désert brings to a close the longest chapter in the life of this survivor from the Century of Light. It existed more than fifty years in ruin, compared to a mere fifteen as a horticultural experiment station, a gentleman's club, and an architectural showplace. In the future that now lies before it, the Désert will of necessity have a different meaning from the one it has possessed. This is the occasion, then, to ask what the meaning has been. What is the essence of the fascination this place has exerted over so many generations of artists and thinkers? For it has been as a stimulation to the imagination, an occasion for art, that the Désert retained its influence after the Monville years were over.

Since then, abandoned by the merrymakers and connoisseurs, stripped of its allusive architectural embellishments and luxurious fittings, the Désert could no longer function as a theater in the way it had in the 1780s, when such gardens were stage sets for the enactment of fantasies of a pastoral or mythic character. The detailed backgrounds provided by the landscape artist left little to the imaginations of the actors, whose parts were in effect dedicated to them by the setting. Such was not the case for visitors to the Désert in its denuded condition, when it had become a skeleton of its earlier self, evoking for Hans Arp, for example, "the white hair of stone." Pale and purified, it was a screen on which could be projected whatever the artists wished to see. Part of the fascination of the Désert lies in observing how radically these wishes have changed with the centuries.

If for its eighteenth-century admirers the fully realized garden was a triumph of artifice, for the twentieth century it has represented the opposite: the defeat of the artist's will by the superior power of time and nature. By their contemporaries, picturesque gardens such as the Désert were appreciated for their ingenious integration of the civilizing arts, as works that incorporated the techniques of painting, sculpture, architecture,

horticulture, and engineering with the content of literature. Its effects were most appreciated when they met the standard of verisimilitude. Thus the newly constructed Chinese House was praised insofar as it was considered faithful to its models in oriental architecture. If the Emperor of China "would acknowledge it," as the Prince de Ligne asserted, it was a success. Similarly, Laborde singled out for praise the views at the Désert that most closely resembled the work of the great landscape painters. His otherwise damning description commends Monville for "having known how to play with light and shadow well enough to create the noble dim light of Ruysdael and Poussin."[81] Blaikie and others reserved their enthusiasm for how powerfully the Broken Column evoked its literary analog, the Tower of Babel in the Bible.

In the twentieth century, on the contrary, writers and artists were enchanted by the Désert as a symbol of the defeat of man's intelligence by forces that are primitive, elemental, and irrational. Such was the sensibility of those adventurous enough to "break in through the crumbling wall," in the words of Choppin de Janvry, such as André Breton, Jacques Prévert, Cyril Connolly, Elsie de Wolfe, Olga Carlisle, and the photographers Jerome Zerbe, Suzanne La Font, Geoffrey James, and Michael Kenna. For these artists it was the presence of unbridled nature that fascinates.

One afternoon in 1945, Cyril Connolly watched "goats clattering up the beautifully undulating spiral staircase" of the Column and "fell hopelessly in love with the place."[82] Of course, it is Colette who writes most effusively of nature's ascendancy at the Désert. Delighting in its ruined state as a testimony to the devouring vigor of plant life, she exaggerates the sentiments of all the visitors who have applauded the revenge of nature, including Sirén, who delights at the spectacle of "exuberant vegetation" entwining itself through the windows of the "Castle of Sleeping Beauty," as he calls the Column.

As a shrine to the primitive, the Désert had moved closer to its Greek inspirations, with the Temple of Pan a reminder to the visitor that this trouble-making nature god was now the deity of the place, infusing his "panic" into the atmosphere of the ruined Désert. With her tendency to anthropomorphize, Colette makes explicit the way plant life and architectural monuments had changed roles as the masters of the garden. The monster who casts its shadows over the Désert was no longer the giant Column, but the gigantic trees, "like towers, with their crowns sixty feet from the ground, an unbroken skirt of branches right down to the ground".[83]

With its monstrous trees, its shadows, its air of isolation, the Désert in modern times could be a frightening place, where one ventured seeking the thrills of terror. Colette compares its allure to that of the haunted house. "Today, inside these walls one feels as much legitimate fear as pleasure," she writes. "An armed prowler would not dare to stay here at night. No more than us would he like the chaos of the interior. . . . How to convince yourself that in this dungeon-like darkness, a rosewood headrest and the remains of a commode are not positively evil?"

Evil has its fascination, and to many, the Désert offered a spectacle of the battle between civilization and nature so mesmerizing they could not bear to see it end. Thus the note of ambivalence in so much of the writing by those supporting the restoration of the garden. Colette admits being of two minds about saving it. "Having known the Désert under a stormy June sky, I tremble to see it changed, swept of its debris and blinking in the light of its new cleanliness." She expresses the hope we can share: that its inevitable restoration will not rid the garden of its ghosts, and that M. de Monville's spirit may live on in his Désert.

Section   1.
The Construction of the Désert de Retz,
1774–1789

4. View of the Column, Temple of Pan, Little Altar, and Open-Air Theater. At the request of King Gustavus III of Sweden, Monville sent him a series of ink drawings of follies at the Désert de Retz that included this panorama attributed to the artist Carmontelle, who designed and depicted the Parc Monceau. Known for decades as the "Stockholm drawings," these were executed sometime between the king's visit to the Désert on July 14, 1784, and March 28, 1785. The images are similar to the engravings published by Le Rouge in July, 1785. Louis Carrogis, called Carmontelle, ca. 1785. Brown ink. *Coll:* National Swedish Art Museums.

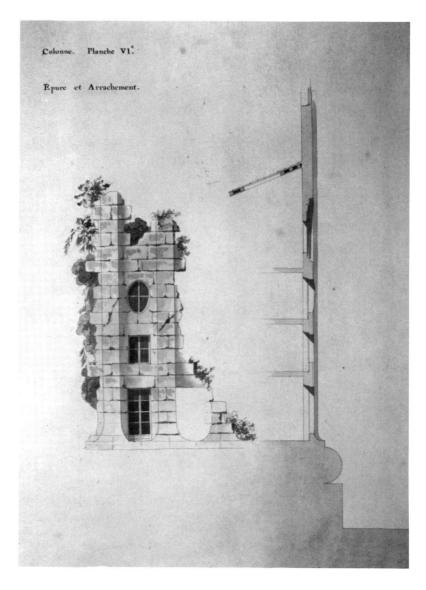

5. The "Stockholm drawing" of the Broken Column section has only four floors, lacking the two basement levels indicated in the *Le Rouge* version. Racine de Monville, ca. 1785. Ink and watercolor. *Coll:* Royal Library, Stockholm.

6. This working drawing of the Broken Column is indistinguishable from the engraving in *Le Rouge.* Racine de Monville, ca. 1785. Ink and watercolor. *Coll:* Royal Library, Stockholm.

7. This brooding image of the Column is unlike the comparable image from Le Rouge. Drawn from a different angle, it has a more dramatic roofline and is wider, showing six bays and windows rather than five. Formerly attributed to François Barbier, the artist was identified in 1986 as the creator of the Désert de Retz. Racine de Monville, ca. 1785. Ink and watercolor. *Coll:* National Swedish Art Museums.

Colonne. Planche VIIe

Élévation Géométrale.

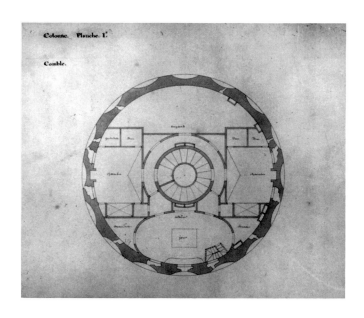

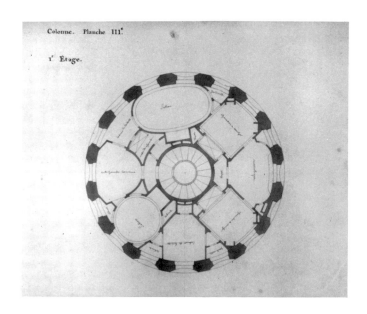

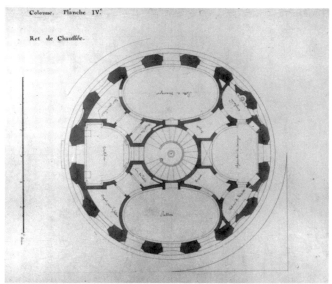

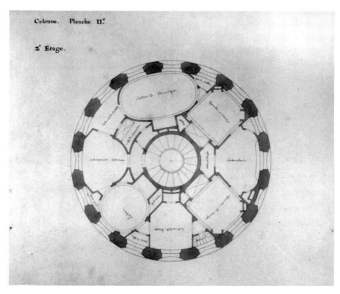

8. Broken Column, plan of ground floor and attic. Racine de Monville, ca. 1785. Ink and watercolor. *Coll:* Royal Library, Stockholm.

9. Plan of first and second floors (the same).

10. Chinese House, section. The decor of the interior is more detailed here than in Le Rouge. Racine de Monville, ca. 1785. Ink and watercolor. *Coll:* National Swedish Art Museums.

Maison Chinoise.   Planche II.

Coupe sur la longueur.

11. Chinese House, elevation on the entry side. The Chinese figures with parasols are not present in the engraving in Le Rouge. Racine de Monville, ca. 1785. Ink and watercolor. *Coll:* National Swedish Art Museums.

12. Chinese House, side elevation.

Maison Chinoise. Planche IV.

Elévation en face. Côté de l' Entrée.

Maison Chinoise. Planche III.

Elévation Latérale.

MAISON DE Mʳ DE MONVILLE
Faubourg Sᵗ Honoré:
COTE DE LA COUR.
Nᵒ 57.

13. Court elevation of the house of M. de Monville in Paris, rue d'Anjou-Saint Honoré, the larger of two designed by Etienne-Louis Boullée, 1764, demolished in the nineteenth century. F. M. Testard, *Paris et la province ou choix des plus beaux monuments d'architecture en France,* Paris, 1790. Engraving. *Coll:* Bibliothèque Nationale, Paris.

14. Plan of legislative chambers in a national capitol building, Thomas Jefferson, 1792. Ink. *Coll:* Massachusetts Historical Society.

15. Plan of the first floor of the rotunda, University of Virginia, Thomas Jefferson, ca. 1821. Ink. *Coll:* University of Virginia Library.

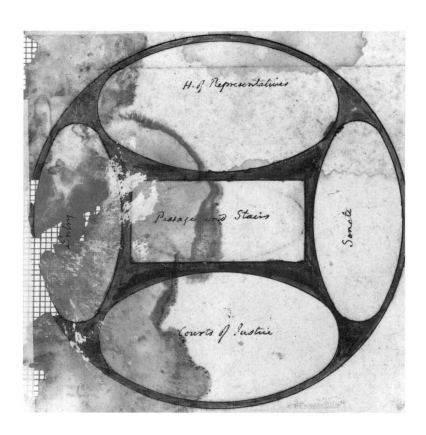

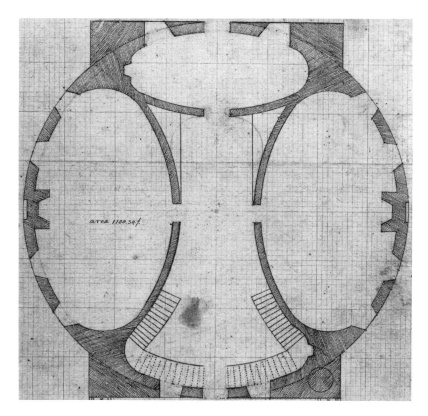

Coupe prise sur A. B.

Plan du 2.ᵉ Etage.

Cabinet   Chambre   Toilette
           à Coucher.

Garde Ro.   Garde Ro.

Salle
de Billard.   Garde Meuble.

Garde Robe. Garde Ro.

Cabinet   Antichambre   Garde Robe.

Plan general.

Krafft.   Boullay.

16. Early nineteenth-century section and floor plans of the Broken Column showing the conical skylight and plantings on the roof. The plans differ slightly from Le Rouge, showing a billiard room on the third floor and no plan for the attic. Boullay, in J. C. Krafft, *Recueil des plus jolies maisons de Paris et de France, d'Angleterre et d'Allemagne,* Paris, 1808–1810. Engraving. *Coll:* Getty Center.

Cah. II.

Pl. 63.

Maison du jardin nommé le désert près la forêt de Marly, bâtie par le propriétaire Mr. Demenville.

Elevation.

Plan du Rez de Chaussée.

Plan du 1er Etage.

17. Early nineteenth-century elevation and floor plans of the Broken Column showing plantings on the roof. Boullay, in J. C. Krafft, *Recueil des plus jolies maisons de Paris et de France, d'Angleterre et d'Allemagne,* Paris, 1808–1810. Engraving. *Coll:* Getty Center.

18. "The Chinese Pavilion in the park of the Désert." Early nineteenth-century view of the Chinese House showing its lake but not the fence, outbuildings, or "Chinese" garden with serpentine paths indicated in Le Rouge. A. L. J. de Laborde, *Descriptions des nouveaux jardins de la France, et des ses anciens châteaux*, Paris, 1808–1815. Engraving. *Coll:* Getty Center.

19. "View of a hamlet in the park named the Désert." Early nineteenth-century engraving giving the only surviving view of the Hamlet, or Commons. A. L. J. de Laborde, *Descriptions des nouveaux jardins de la France, et des ses anciens châteaux*, Paris, 1808–1815. Engraving. *Coll:* Getty Center.

Section 2.
Models from Antiquity and Analogs in
Contemporary Gardens

21. The Temple of Love and rustic bridge at Méréville were designed by the painter Hubert Robert. A. L. J. de Laborde, *Description des nouveaux jardins de la France, et des ses anciens châteaux,* Paris, 1808–1815. Engraving. *Coll:* Getty Center.

20. The Temple of the Sibyl at Tivoli, a much-painted Roman ruin and the model for the ruined hilltop temples at the Désert, Stowe, Méréville, Ermenonville, and other gardens. Unknown artist, 1840. Engraving. *Coll:* Roger-Viollet.

22. Ermenonville, Temple of Modern Philosphy. Osvald Sirén, ca. 1949. Photograph. *Coll:* National Swedish Art Museums.

23. The Temple of Pan before restoration. Michael Kenna, 1988. Photograph. *Coll:* Michael Kenna.

Dom.ᵃ Amici   dis. dal vero   e inc. nel 1833.

Sepolcro di Cajo Cestio

24. The mausoleum of Caius Cestius on the Appian Way inspired eighteenth-century garden pyramids including those at the Désert de Retz and Parc Monceau, as well as the Masonic pyramid that appears on the American dollar bill. Monville owned the Piranesi engravings of this Roman monument. Domenico Amici, 1833. Engraving. *Coll:* Roger-Viollet.

25. The Pyramid at the Parc Monceau, Paris. Unknown artist, ca. 1870. Woodcut. *Coll:* G. B. Carson.

26. The Pyramid at the Désert de Retz was inspired by the Roman monument of Caius Cestius on the Appian Way. Michael Kenna, 1988. Photograph. *Coll:* Michael Kenna.

27. The Pyramid of Maupertuis, with its underground grotto, may have been built as a Masonic lodge in the 1760s at the garden of Elysée on the estate of the Marquis de Montesquiou. It has been attributed both to Brongniart and to Ledoux, who designed the château. Claude-Louis Châtelet, ca. 1785. Oil on canvas.

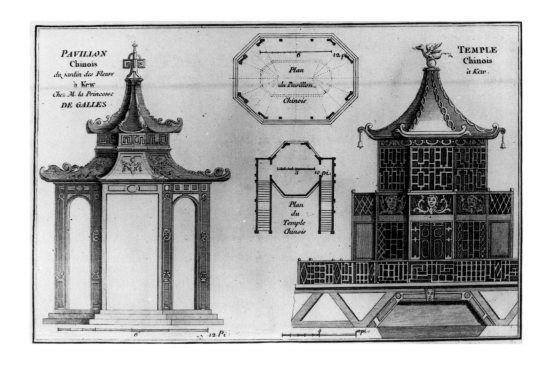

28. The House of Confucius at Kew Gardens outside of London, designed by William Chambers. After William Chambers, ca. 1770. Engraving. *Coll:* Roger-Viollet.

29. The Temple of Mars at the Parc Monceau in Paris. Columns based on actual Roman ruins were a feature of the garden of Monville's friend and Grand Master of the Paris Freemasons, the Duc de Chartres. L. Carrogis, called Carmontelle, *Jardin de Monceau*, Paris, 1779. Engraving. *Coll:* Getty Center.

30. "Turris Babel." This engraving of the Tower of Babel was in the library of the architect Boullée, who has been considered the most likely designer of the Broken Column at the Désert de Retz. I. Cruyl from A. Kircher, Amsterdam, 1679. Engraving. *Coll:* Roger-Viollet.

31. Boullée's unbuilt tower design, thought to be inspired by views of the Tower of Babel that show it encircled by a spiral stair. Etienne-Louis Boulée, 1772. Ink. *Coll:* Bibliothèque Nationale, Paris.

32. The Ruined Tower and bridge at Betz embellish a landscape garden designed by Hubert Robert, considered a candidate for architect of the Désert de Retz. A. L. J. de Laborde, *Description des nouveaux jardins de la France, et des ses anciens châteaux,* Paris, 1808–1815. Engraving. *Coll:* Getty Center.

Constant-Bourgeois del.   Atha. fs Massard sculp.

La RUINE dans le Parc de BETZ.

The RUIN in the Park of BETZ. | Der RUIN im Park zu BETZ.

33. The rusticated stone opening of Dido's Grotto at the Marquis de Girardin's Ermenonville, 1764. Marc Treib, 1981. Photograph. *Coll:* Marc Treib.

34. The heavily rusticated stone entrance to Le Désert de Retz from the Forest of Marly recalls the giant stone porticos in Piranesi's *Carceri* series. On the other side of the gate is the Grotto. Unknown photographer, ca. 1910. *Coll:* Olivier Choppin de Janvry.

35. Prison. The resemblance of the Marly entrance to Piranesi's portal is a reminder that the Désert participates in the megalomania of the age. G. B. Piranesi, *Carceri,* plate 9, 1760. Etching and engraving. *Coll:* Achenbach Foundation for Graphic Arts.

Section 3.
The Désert in the Nineteenth and Twentieth Centuries

36. Nineteenth-century view of the Broken Column showing the cracks and broken roofline, as well as the Cross of St. Andrew associated with Masonic iconography. After Laroque, nineteenth century. Lithograph. *Coll:* Roger-Viollet.

37. The earliest photograph known to have been taken at the Désert, showing the fissures and jagged roof of the Broken Column. Unknown photographer, ca. 1850. *Coll:* Olivier Choppin de Janvry.

38. The earliest-known photograph of the Chinese House. Unknown photographer, ca. 1900. *Coll:* Olivier Choppin de Janvry.

39. An early twentieth-century panorama of the Désert de Retz, showing the Broken Column, Commons (outbuildings), and lake. Unknown
photographer, ca. 1910. *Coll:* Olivier Choppin de Janvry.

40. An early twentieth-century panorama of the Désert de Retz, showing the Chinese House. Unknown photographer, ca. 1910. *Coll:* Olivier
Choppin de Janvry.

41. Members of the Fré-
déric Passy family, who
owned the Désert from
1856 to 1936 and lived in
the Broken Column,
showing their addition of
fourth-story windows and
flattened roof. Harlingue,
ca. 1910. Photograph.
Coll: Roger-Viollet.

42. The Little Altar with
boy, during the Passy
ownership of the Désert.
Unknown photographer,
ca. 1899. *Coll:* Roger-
Viollet.

43. The remains of the false rocks of the Grotto, inside the Marly entrance, with members of Passy family. Harlingue, ca. 1910. Photograph. *Coll:* Olivier Choppin de Janvry.

44. Entrance of the Temple of Repose, showing rusticated columns standing today. Harlingue, ca. 1910. Photograph. *Coll:* Olivier Choppin de Janvry.

45. Owner Frédéric Passy, a winner of the Nobel Peace Prize, at the Model Farm at the Désert de Retz. Unknown photographer, ca. 1900. *Coll:* Roger-Viollet.

46. Interior of the Broken Column during the residence of the Passy family. Harlingue, ca. 1910. Photograph. *Coll:* Roger-Viollet.

47. Interior of the Chinese House. Unknown photographer, ca. 1900. *Coll:* Olivier Choppin de Janvry.

48. The Chinese House. Unknown photographer, ca. 1928. Paul Jarry, *La Guirlande de Paris.* Paris, 1928.

49. The Grotto entry from inside the garden looking out toward the Forest of Marly. Osvald Sirén, ca. 1949. Photograph. *Coll:* National Swedish Art Museums.

50. A third-floor window of the Broken Column, showing the oval shutters and original marble fireplace. Osvald Sirén, ca. 1949. Photograph. *Coll:* National Swedish Art Museums.

51. View of the Broken Column. Osvald Sirén, ca. 1949. Photograph. *Coll:* National Swedish Art Museums.

52. The overgrown Gothic Church. Osvald Sirén, ca. 1949. Photograph. *Coll:* National Swedish Art Museums.

53. The overgrown Pyra-
mid. Osvald Sirén, ca.
1949. Photograph. *Coll:*
National Swedish Art
Museums.

54. The Chinese House existed in decay until 1972, when it collapsed into the lake. Osvald Si-rén, 1949. Photograph. *Coll:* National Swedish Art Museums.

55. André Breton and his Surrealist group in front of the St. Germain gate of the Désert de Retz. Denise Bellon, 1960. Photograph. *Coll:* Denise Bellon.

Section 4.
The Restoration of the Désert de Retz,
1972–1993

56. The Open-Air Theater seen from the Temple of Pan. Michael Kenna, 1988. Photograph. *Coll:* Michael Kenna.

57. The Broken Column from the Forest of Marly. Michael Kenna, 1993. Photograph. *Coll:* Michael Kenna.

58. The Broken Column, Michael Kenna, 1988. Photograph. *Coll:* Michael Kenna.

59. The oldest tree in the garden, a 450-year-old linden with the Broken Column in the background. Michael Kenna, 1988. Photograph. *Coll:* Michael Kenna.

60. The Temple of Pan
seen from the meadow.
Michael Kenna, 1988.
Photograph. *Coll:* Michael
Kenna.

61. The Pyramid after its restoration. Michael Kenna, 1988. Photograph. *Coll:* Michael Kenna.

62. The restored Pyramid
from back. Michael
Kenna, 1988. Photograph.
Coll: Michael Kenna.

63. The unrestored Gothic Church. Michael Kenna, 1988. Photograph. *Coll:* Michael Kenna.

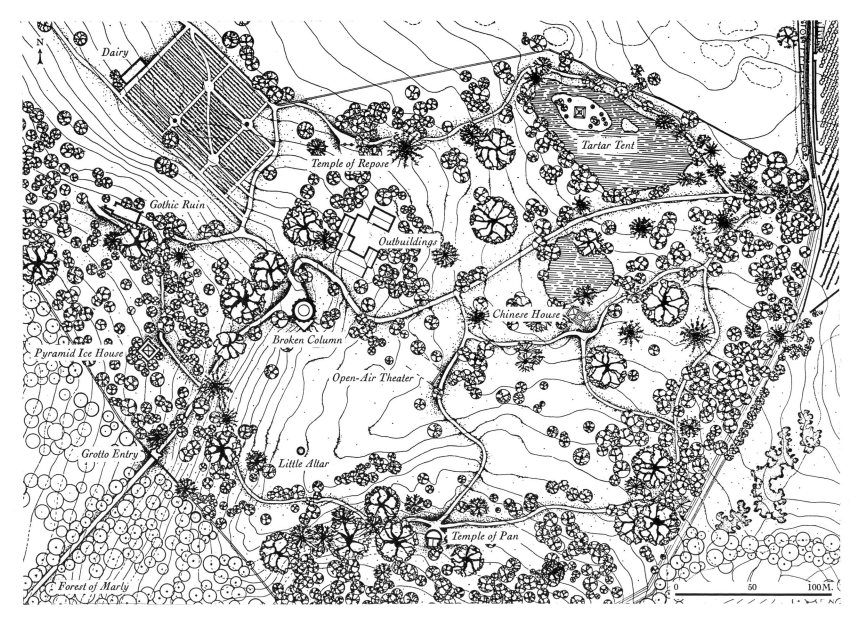

Dairy

Temple of Repose

Tartar Tent

Gothic Ruin

Outbuildings

Broken Column

Chinese House

Pyramid Ice House

Open-Air Theater

Grotto Entry

Little Altar

Temple of Pan

Forest of Marly

0   50   100 M.

64. Map of the Désert de Retz, showing its boundaries and the locations of the surviving monuments in 1989. Off the map are the Model Farm, Hermitage and Obelisk (to the northwest), and the Tomb (to the north). The planned golf course is off the map to the north. *Coll:* Olivier Choppin de Janvry.

65. The unrestored Grotto. Marion Brenner, 1993. Photograph.
Coll: Marion Brenner.

66. The restored Tartar
Tent reflected in the Isle
of Happiness. Michael
Kenna, 1990. Photograph.
Coll: Michael Kenna.

67. The restored meadow
and stream with the Little
Altar on the left and Temple of Pan on the hill at
right. Marion Brenner,
1993. Photograph. *Coll:*
Marion Brenner.

68. The restored circular stairway and skylight in the Broken Column. Marion Brenner, 1993. Photograph. *Coll:* Marion Brenner.

69. The restored kitchen garden of the Model Farm two years after being planted. Marion Brenner, 1993. Photograph. *Coll:* Marion Brenner.

70. The partly restored Temple of Repose with plantings for the walls. Marion Brenner, 1993. Photograph. *Coll:* Marion Brenner.

71. The unrestored Commons. Marion Brenner, 1993. Photograph. *Coll:* Marion Brenner.

72. Restoration architect Olivier Choppin de Janvry, co-owner of the Désert de Retz, in front of the unrestored Temple of Pan. Marion Brenner, 1993. Photograph. *Coll:* Marion Brenner.

73. The completely restored Column exterior, with the cracks and jagged roofline back in place. Marion Brenner, 1993. Photograph. *Coll:* Marion Brenner.

Plates from Le Rouge

Le Désert de Retz as recorded in the twenty-six plates of *Jardins anglo-chinois* by Georges Le Rouge, Cahier XIII, Paris, 1785.

Nouveaux jardins à la mode, published by Georges Louis Le Rouge in Paris from 1776 through 1787, is the grandest illustrated work on garden design in the eighteenth century. Twenty-one parts are devoted to the series *Jardins anglo-chinois.* Begun when the English landscape garden was becoming more fashionable than the traditional French formal garden, Le Rouge claimed that the origin of the new style was the Chinese and that the English irregular garden was its heir, whence came the term *jardins anglo-chinois.* Nearly five hundred engravings document gardens in England, France, Germany, and China, including Stone and Kew, Monceau and Ermenonville. One complete cahier, the thirteenth and largest in the series, issued in 1785, is devoted to the Désert de Retz. All twenty-six plates are reproduced at half-scale. Georges Le Rouge, *Jardins anglo-chinois,* Cahier XIII, Paris, 1785. Engravings. *Coll:* G. B. Carson.

XIII.ᴱ CAHIER

DES JARDINS ANGLO-CHINOIS

Contenant

Les détails du Désert, Jardin Pittoresque à une Lieue de S.ᵗ Germain en Laye,

appartenant à M.ʳ de Monville, Projetté Dessiné et exécuté dans toutes ses parties

Par lui Même. En 26 Planches.

A PARIS

Chez Le Rouge, Ingenieur Géographe du Roi, rüe des Grands Augustins.

Juillet 1785. Prix 12.ᵗᵗ

74. Title page describing the Désert as designed and executed by M. de Monville himself.

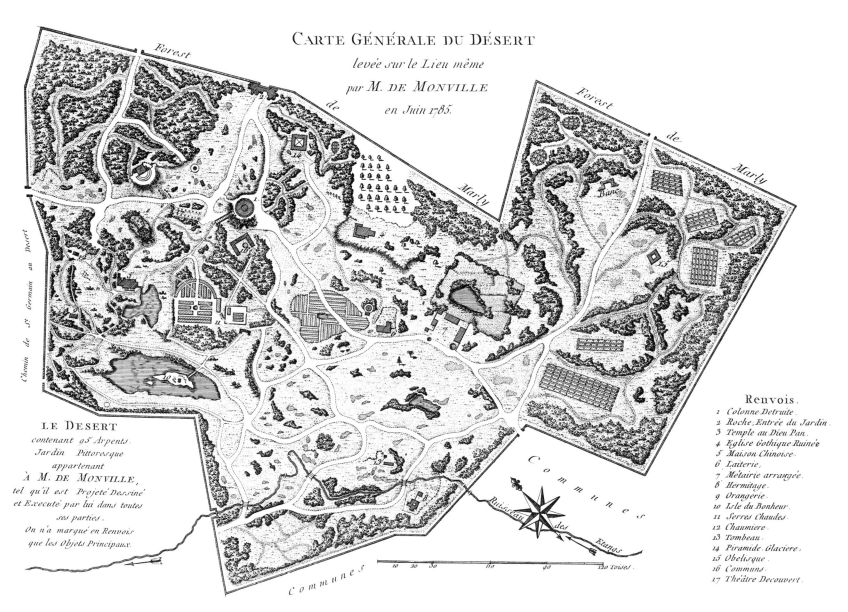

CARTE GÉNÉRALE DU DÉSERT

levée sur le Lieu même

par M. DE MONVILLE

en Juin 1785.

LE DESERT

contenant 95 Arpents.
Jardin Pittoresque
appartenant

À M. DE MONVILLE,

tel qu'il est Projeté Dessiné
et Exécuté par lui dans toutes
ses parties.
On n'a marqué en Renvois
que les Objets Principaux.

Renvois.

1 *Colonne Detruite.*
2 *Roche, Entrée du Jardin.*
3 *Temple au Dieu Pan.*
4 *Eglise Gothique Ruinée.*
5 *Maison Chinoise.*
6 *Laiterie.*
7 *Métairie arrangée.*
8 *Hermitage.*
9 *Orangerie.*
10 *Isle du Bonheur.*
11 *Serres Chaudes.*
12 *Chaumiere.*
13 *Tombeau.*
14 *Piramide Glaciere.*
15 *Obelisque.*
16 *Communs.*
17 *Théâtre Decouvert.*

75. General map of the Désert dated June 1785. Not indicated on the key are the Tartar Tent, Temple of Repose, Rustic Bridge, and Little Altar, although these follies are depicted in the plates.

ROCHER
vûe.
de l'interieur
du Jardin
Faisant l'Entrée
DU DESERT
par la Forêt de Marly.

Gravé par Michel

76. The Grotto entrance seen from inside the Marly wall. The two
torch-bearing satyrs, which were made of tin, were found in storage
after the Revolution. The engraving by Michel is the only signed plate
in the series.

Vue Perspective de la Colonne.

77. Perspective of the Broken Column.

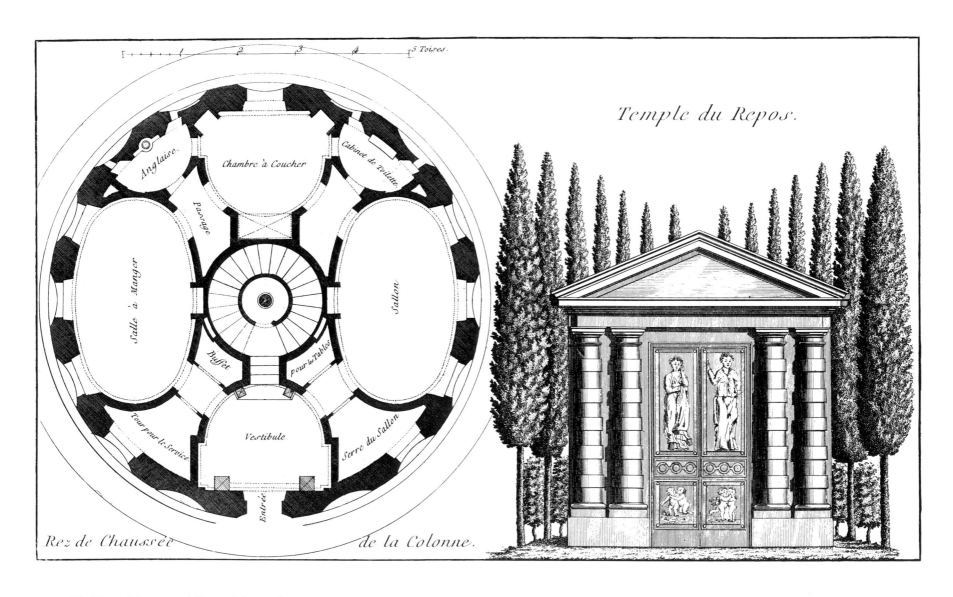

Temple du Repos.

Rez de Chaussée   de la Colonne.

78. Plan of the ground floor of the Broken Column (left); the Temple of Repose (right).

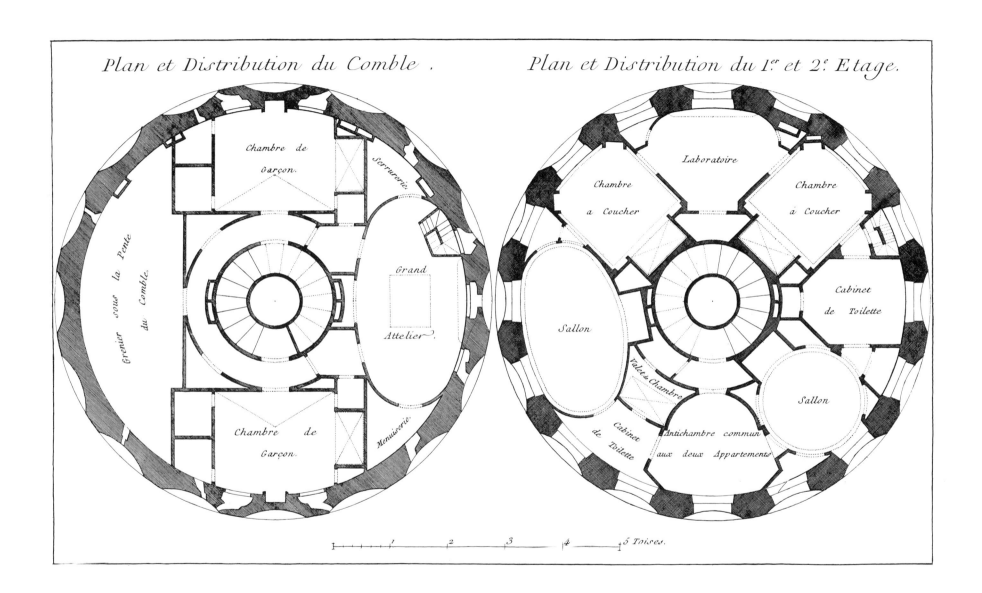

Plan et Distribution du Comble.

Plan et Distribution du 1.ᵉʳ et 2.ᵉ Etage.

Chambre de Garçon.

Serrurerie.

Grenier sous la Pente du Comble.

Grand Attelier.

Menuiserie.

Chambre de Garçon.

Laboratoire.

Chambre à Coucher

Chambre à Coucher

Cabinet de Toilette

Sallon

Valet de Chambre

Sallon

Cabinet de Toilette

Antichambre commun aux deux Appartements

1   2   3   4   5 Toises.

79. Plans of the second and third floors and attic of the Broken Column.

99

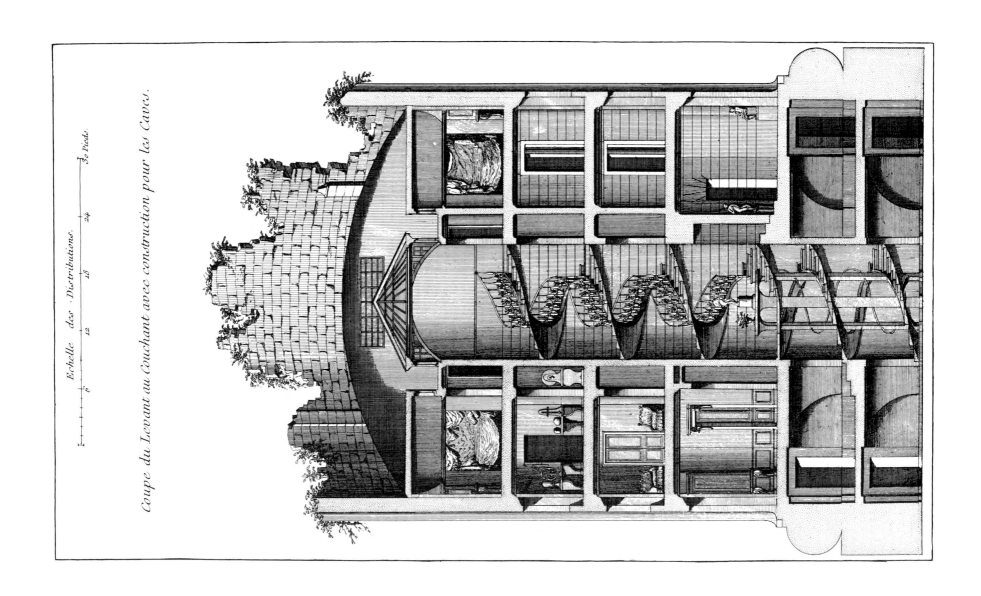

Échelle des Distributions.

Coupe du Levant au Couchant avec construction pour les Caves.

80. Cross-section of the Broken Column.

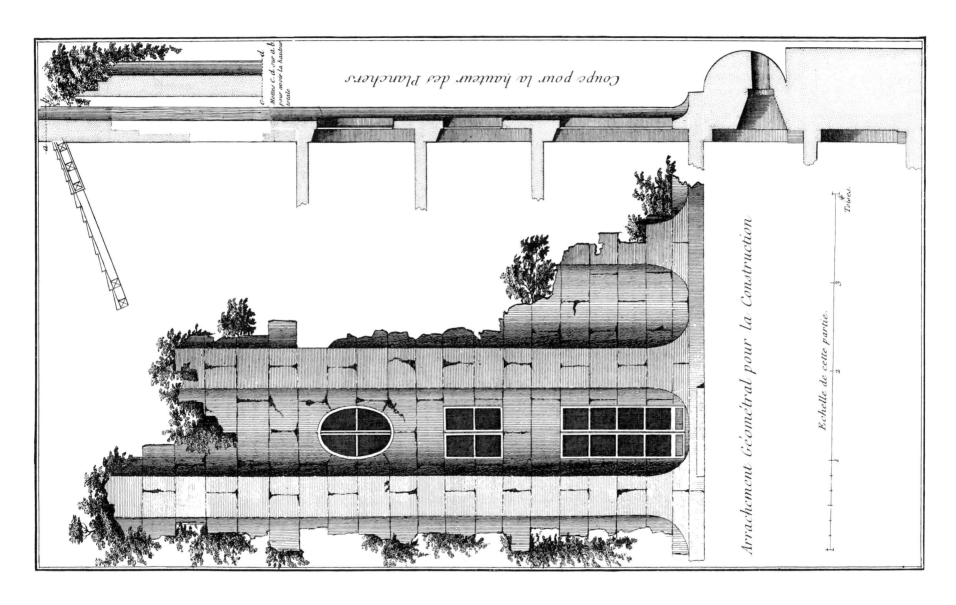

Coupe pour la hauteur des Planchers

Mettes C d. sur a b. pour avoir la hauteur totale

Arrachement Géométral pour la Construction

Echelle de cette partie.

Toises.

81. Elevation of the Broken Column showing the relative heights of the four floors.

Pont Pittoresque qui conduit de la Colonne au Jardin bas.

82. The Rustic Bridge connecting the Broken Column and the lower
garden.

Porte dans le Jardin de la Maison Chinoise.   *Théâtre Decouvert sous un Berceau de Grands Ormes.*

83. A gate in the garden of the Chinese House (left); the Open-Air
Theater under a bower of elms (right).

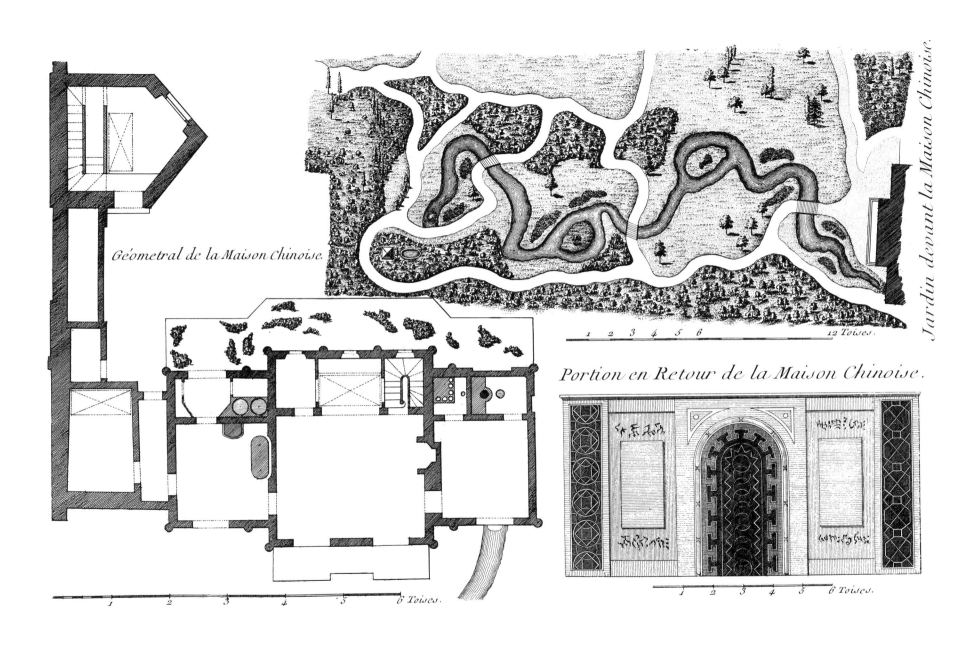

Géometral de la Maison Chinoise.

Jardin devant la Maison Chinoise.

1 2 3 4 5 6   12 *Toises.*

Portion en Retour de la Maison Chinoise.

1 2 3 4 5 6 *Toises.*

1 2 3 4 .5 6 *Toises.*

84. Plans and elevations of the Chinese House and its garden.

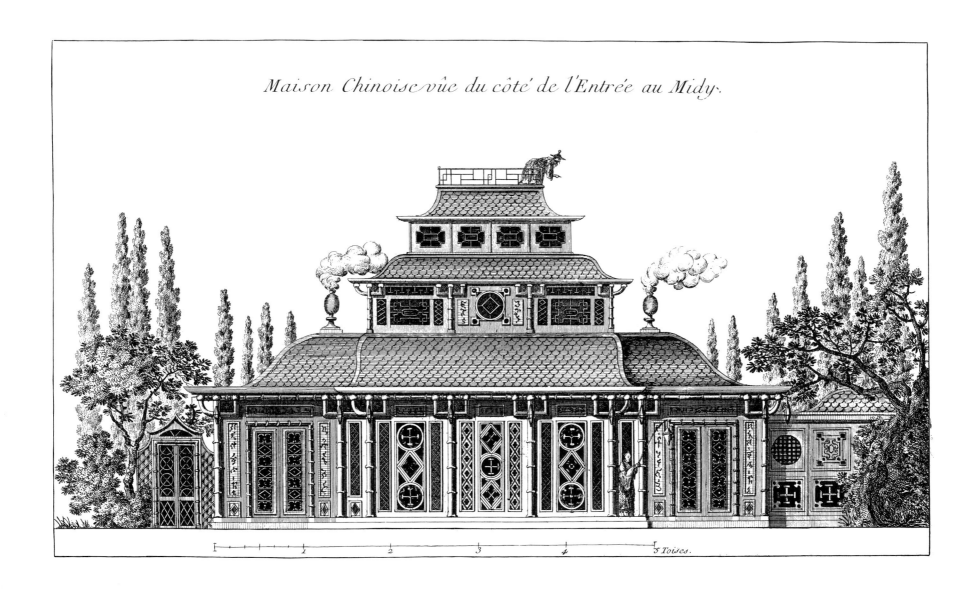

Maison Chinoise vûe du côté de l'Entrée au Midy.

85. The Chinese House seen from the entry side.

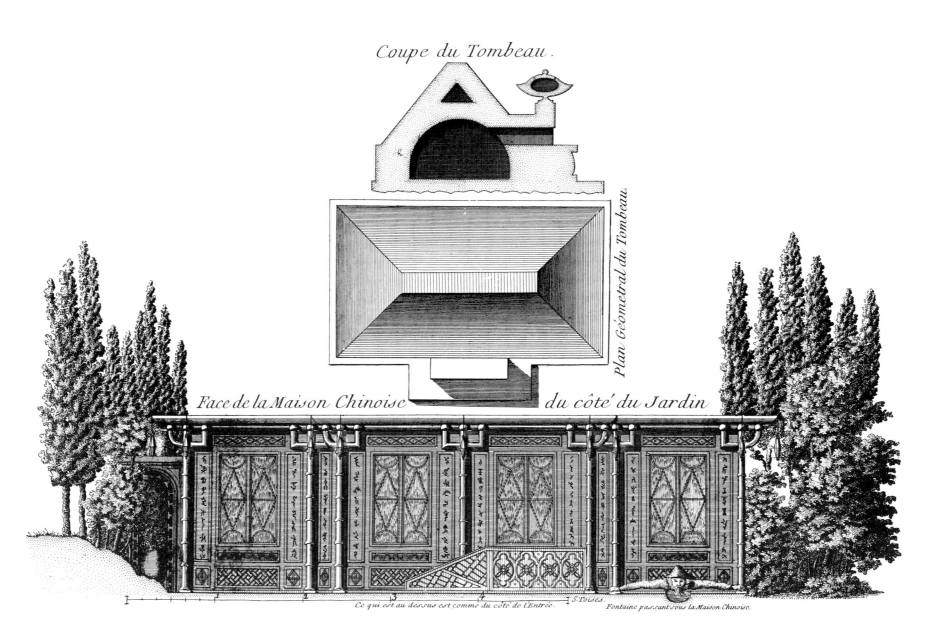

Coupe du Tombeau.

Plan Géometral du Tombeau.

Face de la Maison Chinoise   *du côté du Jardin*

Ce qui est au dessus est comme du côté de l'Entrée.   *5 Toises.*   *Fontaine passant sous la Maison Chinoise.*

86. Plan and section of the Tomb (top); ground floor façade of the
Chinese House on the garden side (bottom).

La Maison Chinoise vûe du côté du Couchant.

87. The Chinese House seen from the west.

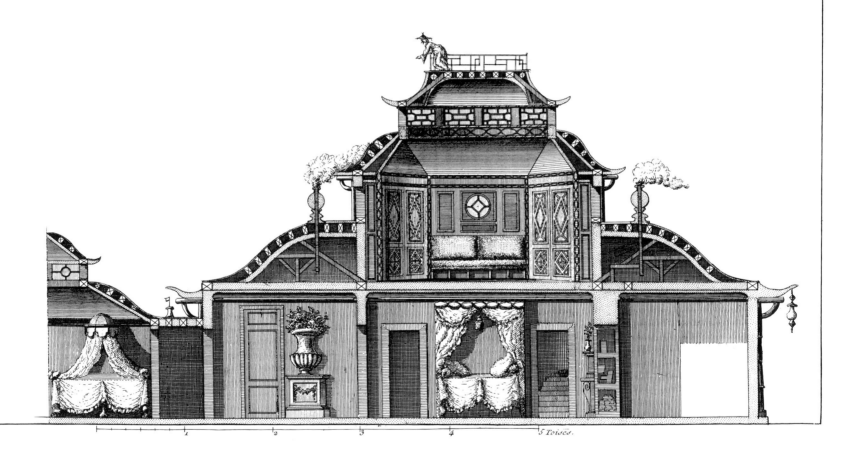

Coupe de la Maison Chinoise sur la Largeur en Face du Jardin.

88. Cross-section of the Chinese House from the garden side.

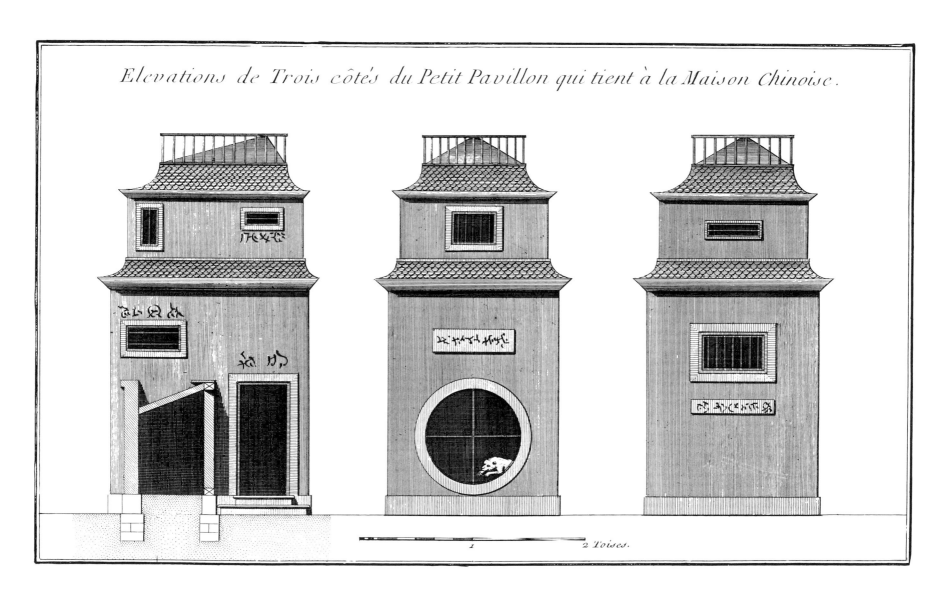

Elevations de Trois côtés du Petit Pavillon qui tient à la Maison Chinoise.

1 2 Toises.

89. Three elevations of the Little Pavilion belonging to the Chinese House.

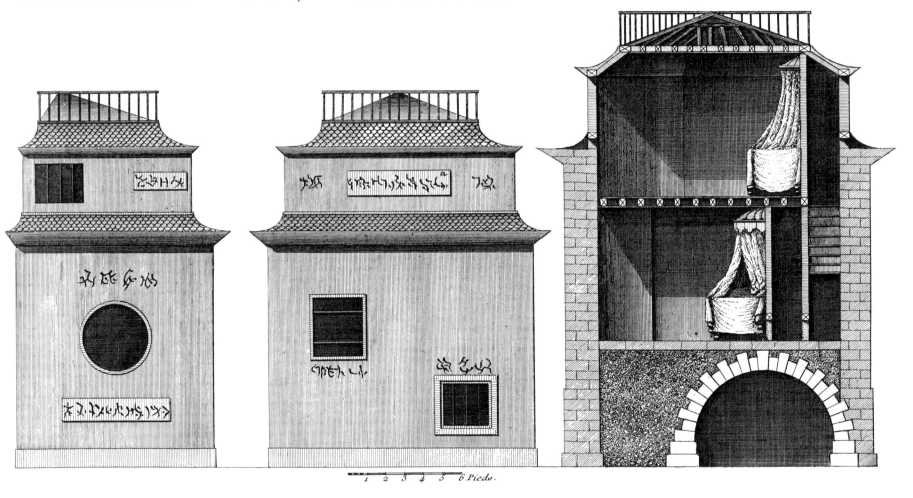

Elevations des deux côtés du Pavillon qui tient à la Maison Chinoise.

Coupe du dit Pavillon.

1 2 3 4 5 6 *Pieds.*

90. Elevations and cross-section of the Little Pavilion at the Chinese
House.

Côté du Nord de la Ruine. | *Eglise Gotique Ruinée vue de Face.*

Elevations qui tiennent à la Maison Chinoise.

1   2   3   4 *Toises.*

91. The Gothic Church from the front and from the north (top); elevations of the Chinese House (bottom).

Petit Autel presque Ruiné.

Grande Porte du Jardin de la Maison Chinoise

92. The partly ruined Little Altar (left); the main gate of the garden of
the Chinese House (right).

Obelisque,
dans la partie moin[...]soignée de la Maitairie

Chaumiere dans le Jardin de la Maison Chinoise.

93. The Obelisk (left); the thatched-roof cottage in the garden of the
Chinese House (right).

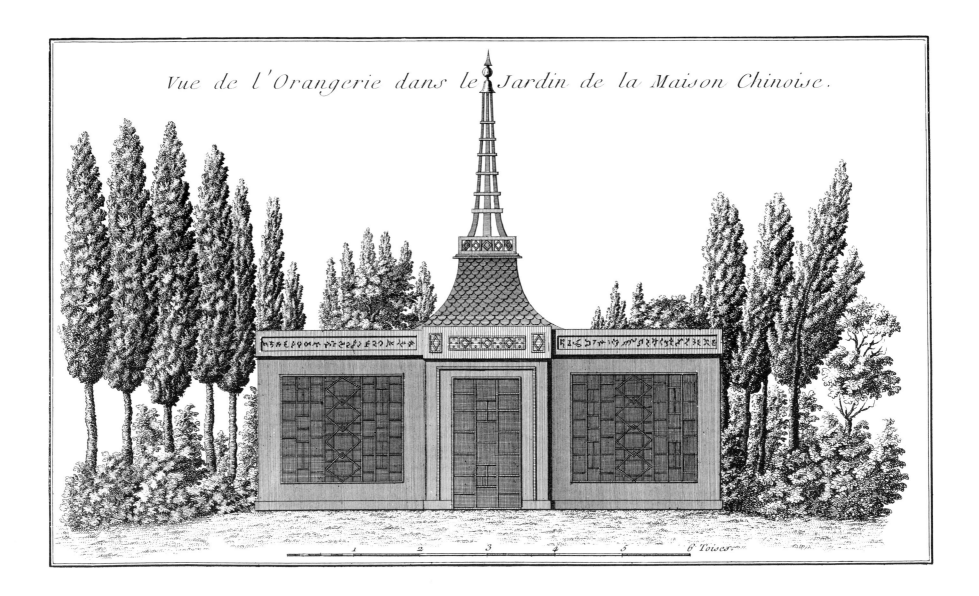

Vue de l'Orangerie dans le Jardin de la Maison Chinoise.

94. The Orangery in the garden of the Chinese House.

Vûe de la Serre pour les Fleurs.

95. The flower greenhouse.

Vûe d'un Treillage en Architecture arrangée.

96. The trellis.

Temple au Dieu Pan.

97. The Temple of Pan.

Vùe du Tombeau.

Tente.

Petite Porte de la Maison Chinoise

Porte de la Tente.

98. Views of the Tomb (top left); the Tartar Tent (bottom left);
the small gate of the Chinese House (right).

Vue de la Glaciere.

99. The Icehouse Pyramid.

Vue de la Glaciere.

99. The Icehouse Pyramid.

Afterword

Olivier Choppin de Janvry

It is nearly thirty years since I entered the Désert de Retz for the first time, through a break in the crumbling wall. I knew it by name only, and that thanks to one of my friends, Arnaud de Lamine, who agreed to take me there one day. Wanting me to be completely surprised, he had not told me about this strange place during our many tramps in the Forest of Marly.

As a young architecture student at the Ecole des Beaux Arts in Paris, a bit on the contentious side, I was looking for a monument to study that would confound the pretensions of my teachers. At that time, during the Algerian War, Palladio, the virtuoso architect of the Renaissance, and Ledoux and Boullée, the visionary architects of the eighteenth century, were forbidden subjects. These masters were too original for our professors, and unhappy were those of us who dreamed of imitating them.

I found my monument at the Désert de Retz, in the house built in the foot of a colossal ruined column. Once habitable but now invaded by vegetation, the barely visible but powerfully scaled column intrigued me. After the first minutes of stupor and astonishment, I vowed to know more about this strange place, and about its creator, M. de Monville.

I wandered through the empty garden, abandoned by its owners since 1936, searching for revealing clues, precious bits of evidence. I took the measurements of the buildings (which are used in today's restoration). My reading led me to discover the refined art of the *jardin anglo-chinois*, in which everything is a symbiosis among the many and varied references to different periods and continents.

The archives of Yvelines revealed their secrets. How thrilling to come upon references to busts of Washington and Franklin in the inventories of the Désert. How exciting it was to study the records of the lawsuit between M. de Monville and the pseudoarchitect Barbier. For an architect, it was an extraordinary way to get to know the genesis of this garden, through the give-and-take between an inspired creator and a competent executor. This information had to be placed in its literary, artistic, and political milieu. I discovered the books from or about the eighteenth century that have now been my bedtime reading for thirty years.

During the years of my education, the Désert was my lifeline. From an indifferent student of classical architecture, I had become an activist of the Désert de Retz, a historian of the gardens of the Century of Light, and soon an assistant to my colleague in the department of Historic Monuments. Aided by Bruno de Saint Victor, I approached the Ministry of Culture to convince it to intervene. Once alerted, the Minister of Culture, André Malraux, took the saving of the Désert in hand. In 1966 he modified the "Law Concerning Historic Monuments" to require careless or destructive owners to participate with the government in financing repairs of historic properties.

From 1972 to 1980 there were several bouts of work to save the Désert that had no goal beyond halting the process of decay. In 1981 the Désert passed into new hands.

My friend Jean-Marc Heftler and I decided to join forces to bring this about. We succeeded in convincing the new owners that they had a mission, and for a token sum they turned the Désert over to us. The gardeners Pierre and Maud Dupas joined us in the work of renewing the Désert, giving up their beautiful country place at Quercy and their hanging gardens at the base of the valley of la Petite Seonne. That was in 1988. For the first time in fifty years, owners of the Désert were happy to work on the property. Life was about to take hold again at the Désert.

One of our problems has been the fact that the Désert ought to be open to all. Monsieur de Monville gave whoever asked him a ticket to visit the garden and I believe that he was right. A *jardin philosophic* is not a commercial enterprise. It is a fragile environment that cannot withstand great traffic. Yet we believe that it would be a mistake to wait until the restoration is finished before letting in the public. Often it is the process of restoration more than the restoration itself that interests visitors. One can have misgivings about a restoration that seems to have been completed in secret.

For the interest of a historic garden is its continuity, not its original state. Should we dig up the border of the Pyramid and plant a symmetrical row of poplars as shown in the Le Rouge engraving of 1785 or should we preserve the extraordinary leafy canopy made up of chestnuts and lindens? Should one restore by the letter or in the spirit of the original, or with wit?

To restore a historic park, one must understand it from the inside. Then one strives to revive all its components and make them live again in harmony, to recommence a process of continuous creation. Architecture has always been one of the essential components of the Art of the Garden. In fact, as Monique Mosser has remarked, the two have rarely been dissociated. And for Candide, the hero of Voltaire's story, to be able to "cultivate his garden," certain historical conditions must be fulfilled. Hirschfield is right to underline that "one seeks the traces of the Art of the Garden only in those eras that have been civilized, enlightened, peaceful."

But gardens also exist in our collective subconscious. The garden was man's first domain, and in the course of the centuries he gave it numerous names meaning the Earthly Paradise, Eden. The hanging gardens of Babylon were one of the seven wonders of the world, the only one that we never forget, even though we have no description of it. Our efforts to recreate it always remain works of the imagination.

Notes

1. This classic statement of the aims of the picturesque garden was made by the artist Louis Carrogis (Carmontelle) in defense of his eclectic array of follies at Monceau, built at the same time as the Désert de Retz. Prospectus to *Jardin de Monceau*, p. 2. A profusion of historical definitions of picturesque garden types based on their formal features was codified for modern readers by Dora Weibenson in her comprehensive 1978 study, *The Picturesque Garden in France*. Recently, however, these categories have been challenged by a generation of historians interested in the intentions of individual garden owners. For an introduction to the concepts of the amateur garden, the occult park, and the psychological garden, see Manfredo Tafuri's *Teorie e storia dell'architettura* and the work of the Swedish scholar Magnus Olausson and Monique Mosser in France.

2. Ligne, *Coup d'oeil sur Beloeil*, p. 222.

3. Sirén, *China and Gardens of Europe of the Eighteenth Century*, p. 116.

4. Colette and Izis-Bidermanas, *Paradis terrestre*, pp. 59–82.

5. The cause of Monville's death in April 1797 was reported as gangrene from an abcess of the gums. In 1793 he had been called twice before the revolutionary tribunal but did not appear. He was released after 9 Thermidor. Archives Nationales, O 1492 F^7 4573, 4574^{51}.

6. Watelet, *Essai sur les jardins*, p. 60.

7. Walpole, "The History of the Modern Taste in Gardening," in Isabel Chase, *Horace Walpole: Gardenist*, pp. 22–23. Walpole's satirical note on French gardens, added to the 1782 edition, is a comic masterpiece among eighteenth-century garden writing. Watelet could well be the intended victim in Walpole's mocking portrait of the proprietor so concerned with moral improvement that he decorates his landscape not only with "temples and Chinese pagodas" but with "schools and foundling hospitals." Walpole chides the French for both misunderstanding the spirit of English gardens they are imitating and refusing to admit they are in fact imitating them, "ascribing our discoveries to the Chinese, or calling our taste in gardens Le Gout Anglo-Chinoise." Walpole is merciless in his ridicule of the term *jardin anglo-chinoise* and was instrumental in curbing its usage in England. However, he offers a plausible explanation for its rise in France: the fact that the English theorist Whateley's *Observations on Modern Gardening* and Chambers' *Dissertation on Oriental Gardens* appeared in French translations within a few years of each other, in 1770 and 1772. Walpole's note is based on his tour of French gardens in 1771, too early, unfortunately, for him to have included a witty comment on the Désert de Retz.

8. Arthaud, *Enchanted Visions*, p. 247.

9. This often-told story is recounted in detail in Montgaillard, *Souvenirs*, pp. 151–152.

10. Laborde, *Descriptions des nouveaux jardins de la France*, pp. 147–150.

11. Ligne, *Coup d'oeil*, p. 222.

12. Laborde, *Descriptions des nouveaux jardins de la France*, p. 147.

13. Jefferson to Maria Cosway, October 12, 1786, *Papers*, 10:443–454. History agrees with Jefferson scholar Jack McLaughlin that this "is one of the notable love letters in the English language," made all the more poignant by the circumstances of its composition. Jefferson wrote it a few days after he had said goodbye to Cosway at the Pavillon Saint Denis gateway out of Paris. Her return to London brought an end to a two-month idyll in which they were together almost daily. He penned its 4,000 words laboriously with his left hand, having broken his right wrist weeks before. Rice believes Jefferson fell when he tried to impress Cosway by jumping a fence on horseback; in Marie Kimball's more prosaic account he "tripped over a large kettle in his own courtyard." Opinions vary as to the nature of Jefferson's relationship with this accomplished beauty, who had made a marriage of convenience with the wealthy and eccentric London society painter Richard Cosway. Evidence supports Rice's view that Jefferson "was infatuated from the moment he saw the exquisite Maria," whom Kimball describes as "delicately voluptuous, with a slight pout and a foreign accent that men found irresistible." They corresponded until Jefferson's death. The engraved portrait she gave him is in the collection at Monticello. See Rice, *Thomas Jefferson's Paris*, p. 20; McLaughlin, *Jefferson and Monticello*, p. 213; Kimball, *Jefferson: The Scene of Europe*, pp. 160–183, and Bullock, *My Head and My Heart: A Little History of Thomas Jefferson and Maria Cosway*.

14. William Howard Adams has pointed out the resemblance between the circular floor plans of the first floor of the rotunda and of the piano nobile of the Broken Column, with its oval salon and dining room on either side of the entry, a smaller semioval room opposite, and intervening space in the shape of a "dumbbell." The larger area of the rotunda allowed the smaller room to be a complete oval. However, no one has noted that Jefferson's floor plan for a capitol building in Washington, D.C., which he offered to the capital's architect L'Enfant, is identical to these in its basic configuration. Jefferson was a believer in the appropriateness of the circular building for public edifices. He never saw Rome and the Pantheon, but during his stay in Paris he admired the largest domed structure in the city, the grain market, the Halle aux Bleds, designed by Legrand and Molinos according to the construction methods of the Renaissance architect Philibert Delorme. Jefferson adapted this inexpensive system of interlocking boards, which he called "sticks and chips," for the dome of his rotunda and argued unsuccessfully for its use for the house of representatives and a federal dock in Washington. Oval rooms were much in fashion in Jefferson's Paris, where he had two oval salons in his rented house the Hôtel de Langeac, designed by Chalgrin. However, the Désert's particular arrangement of ovals within a circle is so distinctive that it could not have been reproduced accidentally. Adams, *The Eye of Thomas Jefferson*, p. 295.

15. See Kimball, *Jefferson: The Scene of Europe*, p. 166.

16. See McLaughlin, *Jefferson and Monticello*, p. 252.

17. *Sequestre des biens des étrangers, Disney Ffytche*. Archives des Yvelines 4 Q 264.

18. Choppin de Janvry, "Avant que ne disparaîsse à jamais le Désert de Retz," p. 40.

19. Plants seized at the Désert de Retz in the years 1792–1794 include mimosas, cotyledons, and rare cinerarias and hydrangeas. Sold at public auction at St. Germain-en-laye were laurels, orange trees, pomegranates, and Buenos Aires currants. Archives de Seine-et-Oise.

20. Bachaumont, *Mémoires secrètes*, Vol XVII, pp. 350–351.

21. Tilly, *Mémoires*, pp. 97–98.

22. Cosway played her own compositions for the harp at musical evenings at her London home, Schomberg House in Pall Mall. Copies of her

published music found among Jefferson's papers in 1938 brought attention to twenty-five letters of their correspondence that were suppressed by his heirs. See Bullock, *My Head and My Heart*, p. viii.

23. Dufort de Cheverny, *Mémoires sur les règnes de Louis XV et Louis XVI et sur la Révolution*, pp. 316–318.

24. Jefferson to Maria Cosway, *Papers*, 10:453.

25. Dufort de Cheverny, *Mémoirs*, p. 317.

26. Vigée-Lebrun, *Mémoirs*, p. 217.

27. Espinchal, *Mémoirs*, quoted in Choppin de Janvry, "Le Désert de Retz," p. 127.

28. Angivilliers, Bibliothèque Nationale, NAF 2765, p. 25.

29. Chamfort, *Oeuvres complètes*, quoted in Connolly and Zerbe, *Les Pavillons*, p. 17.

30. Genlis, *Mémoires sous les règnes de Louis XV et Louis XVI*, pp. 141–142.

31. Bachaumont, *Mémoires secrètes*, Vol XVI, pp. 350–351.

32. Gallet, *Claude-Nicolas Ledoux*, p. 26.

33. Ibid.

34. See Gallet, *Demeures Parisiennes: L'Epoque de Louis XVI*, p. l08.

35. Tilly, *Mémoires*, pp. 97–98.

36. Bachaumont, *Mémoires secretès*, Vol. XVI, p. 350.

37. Blaikie, *Diary of a Scotch Gardener at the French Court at the End of the Eighteenth Century*, pp. 210–211.

38. Dufort de Cherverny, *Mémoires*, p. 318.

39. See Pérouse de Montclos, *Etienne-Louis Boullée*, pp. 16–19.

40. Thiéry, *Guide des amateurs à Paris*, Vol. I, p. 90.

41. Dufort de Cheverny, *Mémoires*, p. 316.

42. Blaikie, *Diary of a Scotch Gardener at the French Court*, p. 210.

43. There were four separate purchases between 1774 and 1785. See Choppin de Janvry, "Le Désert de Retz," p. 131.

44. Blaikie, *Diary of a Scotch Gardener at the French Court*, p. 211.

45. The attribution to Boullée has been perpetuated by Hautecoeur. See *Histoire de l'architecture classique en France*, p. 223.

46. Pérouse de Montclos, *Etienne-Louis Boullée*, p. 17.

47. Ibid.

48. Connolly and Zerbe, *Les Pavillons*, pp. 176–177.

49. Sirén, "Le Désert de Retz," p. 327.

50. Ibid., p. 328.

51. "Estimation des honoraires dus au Sr Barbier Architecte par M. de Monville," April 12, 1780 (Archives Nationales Zij 1059). This document, discovered by Michel Gallet in 1960, is reproduced in full in Choppin de Janvry, "Le Désert de Retz", pp. 138–148.

52. Choppin de Janvry in the preface to Ketcham, *Le Désert de Retz*, p. 9. Unlike Monville, Barbier was trained in architecture, having been a student at the royal Academy in the 1760s. Among his work is the garden of Ledoux's legendary Hôtel de Thélusson, where he executed the former's design. Archives Nationales Zij 967, 1035, 1059.

53. See Olausson, "The Désert de Retz and King Gustavus III of Sweden," pp. 180–187. Of the drawings of the Chinese House, plate II (the section) is in the National Museum, Stockholm (NM, H Z13/1958) while III and IV (elevations) were donated by Fredrik Magnus Piper to the Royal Academy of Fine Arts, Stockholm (Pi-t-Ki 1–2). The drawings of the Column were given to the Royal Library in 1867 by King Charles XV, where they were misidentified as "a project for a ruined column in the garden of Rosersberg," sometime after which Plate VII, the Column elevation, and the Carmontelle view went to the National Museum, Stockholm.

54. Sirén, "The Désert de Retz," p. 332.

55. The Swedish ambassador to France, Stael von Holstein, wrote in a letter dated March 28, 1785, "At the King's request, M. Monville has made a plan of his garden and of the Duc de Chartres' Winter Garden. See to it that the King gives him quite a handsome present." His second letter is dated September 1, 1785, and refers to sending "a selection of views of the Désert and two plans of the garden." The fact that two separate batches of drawings were sent explains the very different style of the Carmontelle, which is the only view we have, and raises the intriguing possibility that other views by significant artists may yet turn up. Upsalla University Library MS F 830f. Monville's letter to Gustavus reads, "Sire, J'ai l'honneur d'envoier a Votre Majesté les plans qu'elle a desiré, et les détails qui ont paru luy plaire, trop heureux qu'elle aie bien voulu permettre que je luy en fasse l'hommage. J'ai rendu le plan general tel qu'il est projeté, et j'y ai joint des changements qui n'étoient pas encore faits, quand Votre Majesté a bien voulu honnorer le Désert de sa présence." Stockholm, National Archives, Skrivleser till Komungen, Gustavus III. The only drawing Monville here refers to as "having made" is a general plan of the garden, which is not among the Swedish holdings. Olausson believes this plan exists, regretting that he "has not been able to find" it. In any case, Monville's expression that he "had made (or rendered)" this plan does not necessarily mean that he himself drew the finished plan, and by extension the other drawings. Any such determination of authorship is handicapped by the absence of drawings in Monville's hand, as well as the scarcity of examples of his handwriting.

56. The drawings of the Désert de Retz were not listed in the inventory of Gustavus's collection made at the time of his death in 1792, suggesting that they had been lent to his architects for study. The resemblance between the Column and the Desprez schemes for an octagonal villa, gothic tower, and Chinese pavillion was taken by Sirén as evidence that Desprez was himself the artist of the "Swedish Drawings," rather than that he imitated them, as Olaussen maintains. See Olaussen, "The Désert de Retz and King Gustavus III of Sweden," pp. 182–187, and Sirén, *China and Gardens of Europe*, pp. 119–120.

57. Olaussen, "The Désert de Retz and King Gustavus III of Sweden," pp. 182, 186.

58. Sirén, *China and Gardens of Europe*, p. 120.

59. Choppin de Janvry, conversation with author in November 1991.

60. Olausson, "Freemasonry, Occultism, and the Picturesque Garden," pp. 422–424.

61. Adams, *The French Garden*, p. 118.

62. See Olausson, "Freemasory, Occultism, and the Picturesque Garden," p. 422.

63. Germany was the site of several landscape gardens known to have been built as settings for Masonic rites: Royal York zurf Freundscahft in Berlin; Aigen near Salzburg, owned by Basil von Amann; and Louisenlund near Schleswig, the summer residence of the Landgrave Charles of Hesse-Cassel. There is growing speculation that such gardens also existed in France and included the Pyramid at the Marquis de Montesquiou's garden of Elysée and the Pavilion and Winter Garden at the Duc de Chartres's Parc Monceau. Vidler's pioneering study "The Architecture of the Lodges" gives the fullest and most balanced account of the Masonic gardens and maintains a distinction between those that can be read as Masonic allegories and those that functioned as settings for Masonic ritual. Vidler is more skeptical than Olausson and Mosser about Freemasonry being the literal determinant of the design of specific gardens, regarding it as one

influence among many. Both Vidler and Olausson believe that Monville was a freemason. Olausson argues that the absence of his name from the rolls of the Duc de Chartres's lodge is meaningless since only seven of its members' names have survived.

64. Ligne, *Coup d'oeil sur Beloeil,* p. 222.

65. July 21, 1792. Record of purchase by Lewis Disney Ffytche from Racine de Monville of a contry house at Retz and its major furnishings. Archives de Seine-et-Oise.

66. Tilly, *Mémoirs,* pp. 97–98.

67. Ibid.

68. Report of the Comité de Sureté. Archives Nationales, F^7 4573, 4574[51].

69. Tilly, *Mémoires,* pp. 97–98.

70. Ibid.

71. Archives de Seine-et-Oise. Transactions at the Désert de Retz recorded for July 21, 1792, October 19, 1793, October 21, 1793, January 24, 1794, April 14, 1794, January 25, 1811, March 10, 1811, September 3, 1811, and August 1, 1817.

72. To this seizure we owe the useful survey made in 1811, which includes the Collet-Duclos map and inventories the significant trees, indicating their location in relation to the follies and other landmarks. It shows that the plan of the park had been simplified since the Le Rouge map of 1785, with an additional area of 9 arpents (10 percent of the property) put in general cultivation, the kitchen garden regularized, and service roads put in. This document has been a key tool in the restoration. Procès-verbal d'estimation dated February 19, 1811, Archives de Seine-et-Oise.

73. Trees from Monville's time and earlier have survived, including 300-year-old sycamores, maples, hornbeams, and lindens. The oldest is a 450-year old linden near the Broken Column. Under the Passy ownership, the working farm enlarged after the Revolution was maintained out of financial necessity. But efforts were also made to conserve the scheme of Monville's landscaping, retaining the outlines of the timberlands and embellishing their borders with cedars, blue cedars, sycamores, copper beeches, and cypresses. Choppin de Janvry, "D'un jardin historique et de l'histoire de sa restauration," p. 10.

74. See Lécuyer and Moreux, "Le Désert de M. de Monville," pp. 119–126.

75. Colette and Izis-Bidermanas, *Paradis terrestre,* p. 80.

76. The restoration is estimated to take fifteen years, five for clearing and repair of the site, and another ten for replanting and reconstruction. The cost of fifteen million francs for the first stage has come from the Ministry of Culture, Undine, the Florence Gould Foundation, the World Monuments Fund, the Amis des Vieilles Maisons Françaises, and private contributors to the Association des Amis du Désert de Retz.

77. Laborde's views have been consulted in the restoration of the perspectives. There is no single set of images to guide the repair of the follies. Le Rouge was followed for the Pyramid, Broken Column, and Tartar Tent. In the case of the planned restoration of the Temple of Pan, however, there are discrepancies between the Carmontelle drawing, which shows a crumbling Roman ruin, the Le Rouge engraving of a pristine Doric peristyle with open arches and statuary at the roofline, and the existing building, an incomplete peristyle in front and a square room in the back, with the arcades filled in and no statues.

78. The meadow grass is a mixture of 30 percent Ray Grass, 65 percent fetuques, and 5 percent fleole. Replanting of the trees will take place at the rate of thirty trees a year, beginning with the thirteen sequoias donated by an American organization in 1979 in honor of Thomas Jefferson's visit to the Désert. In the work of clearing in the first five years of the restoration, the trees and shrubs taken out were mainly volunteer ash, maple, bay, hawthorne, and Portugese laurel, replaced by new plantings of yew, hydrangeas, Chinese thuya, paniculosa and quercyfolia, and antique roses.

79. For an account of the controversy, see Choppin de Janvry, "Lettre du Désert." *Bulletin de la Société des Amis du Désert de Retz*, No. 1, June 1992.

80. The restoration received the 1987 Prix Lajoue de la Demeure Historique, the 1989 first prize of the Chefs d'Oeuvre en Peril d'Antenne II, and the 1993 Carlo Scarpa Prize from the Benetton Foundation (to Olivier Choppin de Janvry).

81. Laborde, *Descriptions des nouveaux jardins de la France*, p. 147.

82. Connolly and Zerbe, *Les Pavillons*, p. 151.

83. Colette and Izis-Bidermanas, *Paradis Terrestre*, p. 80.

Bibliography

Adams, William Howard. *The Eye of Thomas Jefferson.* Washington, D.C.: National Gallery of Art, 1976. (Exhibition catalog.)

———. *The French Garden: 1500–1800.* New York: George Braziller, 1979.

———. "A Hymn to Ruin." *House and Garden,* October 1984.

Archives de la Seine-Maritime. Series E.

Archives de Seine-et-Oise. Documents A 109.

Archives des Yvelines, IV Documents Q 234.

Archives Nationales. Documents F^7 4573, 4574^{51}, O 1492, Zij 967, 1035, 1059.

Arthaud, Claude. *Enchanted Visions: Fantastic Houses and Their Treasures.* New York: Random House, 1972.

Bachaumont, L. *See* Petit de Bachaumont, L.

Baltrusaitis, J. *Aberrations: Quatre essais sur la légende des formes.* Paris: O. Perrin, 1957.

Bibliothèque Nationale, New French Acquisitions 2765.

Blaikie, Thomas (ed. F. Birrell). *Diary of a Scotch Gardener at the French Court at the End of the Eighteenth Century.* London: George Routledge and Son, 1931.

Bullock, Helen Duprey. *My Head and My Heart: A Little History of Thomas Jefferson and Maria Cosway.* New York: G. P. Putnam's Sons, 1945.

Carrogis, Louis (Carmontelle). *Jardin de Monceau, près de Paris, appartenant à S. A. S. Mgr. le duc de Chartres.* Paris, 1779.

Chamfort, S. R. N. *Oeuvres complètes de Chamfort.* Paris, 1808.

Choppin de Janvry, Olivier. "Avant que ne disparaîsse à jamais le Désert de Retz." *L'Oeil,* September 1967.

———. "Le Désert de Retz." *Bulletin de la Société de l'Histoire de l'Art Français.* 1970.

———. *Le XIIIème cahier des jardins anglo-chinois à la mode de Le Rouge.* Réédition. Paris, 1973.

———. "Les jardins promenades au XVIIIe siècle." *Les Monuments historiques de la France*. Paris, 1976.

———. "Monsieur de Monville et Le Désert de Retz." Manuscript, 1977.

———. "Le Désert de Retz: D'un jardin historique et de l'histoire de sa restauration." Manuscript, 1991.

———. "Lettre du Désert," *Bulletin de la Société des Amis du Désert de Retz*, No. 1, June 1992.

Colette, and Izis-Bidermanas, *Paradis terrestre*. Lausanne, 1953.

Conner, Patrick. *Oriental Architecture in the West*. London: Thames and Hudson, 1979.

Connolly, Cyril, and Jerome Zerbe. *Les Pavillons: French Pavilions of the Eighteenth Century*. New York: Norton, 1979.

Dufort, Jean-Nicolas, Cte de Cheverny. *Mémoires sur les règnes de Louis XV et Louis XVI et sur la Révolution*. Paris, 1886.

Gallet, Michel. *Claude-Nicolas Ledoux*. Paris, 1980.

———. *Demeures Parisiennes: L'Epoque de Louis XVI*. Paris, 1964.

Ganay, E. de. "Fabriques aux jardins du XVIIIe siècle." *Gazette des Beaux-Arts*, May–June 1955.

Genlis, Stéphanie-Félicité. *Mémoires: La Cour de Louis XV*. Paris: Perrin, 1990.

Hautecoeur, Louis. *Histoire de l'architecture classique en France*. Vol. 4, Paris: Picard, 1952.

Hervier, D. "Le Désert de Retz, paradis perdu, paradis à ressusciter?" and A. de Labriffe, "Le Désert de Retz: un cas désespéré?" *Vieilles Maisons Françaises*, December 1983.

Jardins en France: 1760–1820. Caisse Nationale des Monuments Historiques. Paris, 1977. (Exhibition catalog.)

Jarry, Paul. *La Guirlande de Paris*. Paris: Contet, 1928.

Jefferson, Thomas (ed. Julian P. Boyd). *The Papers of Thomas Jefferson*. Princeton: Princeton University Press, 1950.

Ketcham, Diana. *Le Désert de Retz: A Late Eighteenth-Century French Folly Garden*. San Francisco: Arion Press, 1990.

Kimball, Marie. *Thomas Jefferson: The Scene of Europe 1784–1789*. New York: Coward-McCann, 1950.

Krafft, J. C. *Plans des plus beaux jardins pittoresques de France, d'Angleterre et d'Allemagne* and *Recueil des plus jolies maisons de Paris et de France, d'Angleterre et d'Allemagne*. Paris, 1808–1810.

Laborde, Alexandre. *Descriptions des nouveaux jardins de la France, et des ses anciens châteaux*. London: Gregg International Publishing, 1971.

Laugier, M. A. *Essai sur l'architecture*. Paris, 1753.

Lécuyer, R., and J.-Ch. Moreux. "Le Désert de M. de Monville." *L'Amour de l'Art*, April 1938.

Le Dantec, Denise, and Jean-Pierre Le Dantec. *Reading the French Garden*. Cambridge, Mass.: The MIT Press, 1990.

Ledoux, Claude-Nicolas. *L'Architecture considérée sous le rapport de l'art, des moeurs et de la législation*. Paris: Perronneau, 1804, 1846 (2 vols.).

Lefévre, L. Eugène. "Le jardin anglais et la singulière habitation du Désert de Retz." *Bulletin de la Commission des Antiquités et des Arts de Seine et Oise*, 1917.

———. "Maison construite dans le jardin nommé le Désert près de la forêt de Marly par le propriétaire M. de Monville." *Bulletin de la Commission des Antiquités et des Arts de Seine et Oise*, 1917.

Le Rouge, G. L. *Jardins anglo-chinois à la mode.* Cahier XIII. Paris, 1785.

Ligne, C. J. L. *Coup d'oeil sur Beloeil et sur une grande partie des jardins de l'Europe.* Paris: Bossard, 1922.

Lockwood, Charles. "Restoring an Eighteenth-Century French Eccentric Garden." *New York Times,* August 21, 1986.

———. "Restoring Désert de Retz, de Monville's Folly Garden." *Preservation News,* November 1986.

Madec, Philippe. *Boullée.* Paris: Hazan, 1986.

McLaughlin, Jack. *Jefferson and Monticello: The Biography of a Builder.* New York: Henry Holt, 1988.

Montgaillard, Abbé Guillaume Honorés Rocques. *Souvenirs.* Paris: Ollendorf, 1895.

Mosser, Monique. "Le Roche et la colonne." *Revue de l'Art,* No. 58–59, 1983.

Mosser, Monique, and Geoffrey James. *Morbid Symptoms: Arcadia and the French Revolution.* Princeton: Princeton Architectural Press, 1986.

Mosser, Monique and Georges Teyssot, eds. *The Architecture of Western Gardens: A Design History from the Renaissance to the Present Day.* Cambridge, Mass.: The MIT Press, 1991.

Olausson, Magnus. "The Désert de Retz and King Gustavus III of Sweden." *Gazette des Beaux-Arts,* May–June 1986.

———. "Freemasonry, Occultism, and the Picturesque Garden Towards the End of the Eighteenth Century." *Art History,* 1985.

Pérouse de Montclos, Jean-Marie. *Etienne-Louis Boullée (1728–1799): Theoretician of Revolutionary Architecture.* New York: George Braziller, 1974.

Petit de Bachaumont, L. *Mémoires secrètes pour servir à l'histoire de la république des lettres en France.* London, 1777–1779.

Rice, Howard. *Thomas Jefferson's Paris.* Princeton: Princeton University Press, 1976.

Rosenau, Helen. *Boullée and Visionary Architecture.* London: Academy Editions, 1975.

Sirén, Osvald. *China and Gardens of Europe of the Eighteenth Century.* New York: Robert Press, 1950.

———. "Le Désert de Retz." *Architectural Review,* November 1949.

Tafuri, Manfredo. *Teorie e storia dell'architettura.* Bari: Laterza, 1968.

Thiéry, Luc-Vincent. *Guide des amateurs à Paris.* Vol. 1. Paris, 1787.

Tilly, Alexandre. *Mémoires de Comte Alexandre de Tilly, pour servir à l'histoire des moeurs de la fin du XVIIIe siècle.* Vol. 1. Paris, 1828.

Touttain, Pierre André. "Un jardin anglais en Seine et Oise." *Congrés des Fédérations des Sociétés Savantes de Seine et Oise,* May 1959.

Valèry, Marie-Françoise. "Le Désert de Retz." *Demeures et Châteaux,* May–June 1987.

Vidler, Anthony. *Claude-Nicolas Ledoux: Architecture and Social Reform at the End of the Ancien Régime.* Cambridge, Mass.: The MIT Press, 1990.

———. "The Architecture of the Lodges: Ritual Form and Associational Life in the Late Enlightenment." *Oppositions,* No. 5, 1984.

———. *The Writing of the Walls: Architectural Theory of the Late Enlightenment.* Princeton: Princeton Architectural Press, 1987.

Vigée-Lebrun, L. E. (trans. Lionel Strachey). *Memoirs of Madame Vigée-Lebrun.* New York: George Braziller, 1988.

Walpole, Horace. "The History of the Modern Taste in Gardening," in I. Chase, *Horace Walpole, Gardenist*. Princeton: Princeton University Press, 1943.

Watelet, C. H. *Essai sur les jardins*. Paris: Prault, 1774.

Weiler, K., and V. Soyez. "Le Désert de Retz." *Décoration Internationale*, March 1986.

Wiebenson, Dora. *The Picturesque Garden in France*. Princeton: Princeton University Press, 1978.

Index